A MESSAGE FOR MY CHILDREN

"Remember your name when we are sold"
"The Struggles of Mariana McCalister"

Sheila McCalister

Copyright © 2014 Sheila McCalister

All rights reserved. No part of this book may be reproduced, copied, stored, or transmitted in any form or by any means-graphic, electronic, or mechanical including photocopying, recording, or information storage and retrieval systems with the prior written permission of author.
For permission requests, write to the publisher.

Printed in the United States of America

First Printing, 2014

ISBN 978-0-692-24384-8

LuLu Publishing

Library of Congress Control Number: applied for

A MESSAGE FOR MY CHILDREN
"Remember your name when we are sold"
"The Struggle of Mariana McCalister"

Carter Goodwin-Woodson Father of Black History states:

"If Race has no history, it has no worthwhile history tradition, it becomes a negligible factor in the thought of the world, and it stands in danger of being exterminated".

Sheila McCalister

Table of Contents

FOREWORD 6
ACKNOWLEDGEMENTS 8
CHAPTER 1 OUR BEGINNING… 10
CHAPTER 2 THE RATLIFF'S 12
CHAPTER 3 SLAVE RECORDS 19
CHAPTER 4 MARIANA'S LIFE 28
CHAPTER 5 CAROLINE RATLIFF MCCALISTER ... 33
CHAPTER 6 SANDY MCCALISTER 37
   Marriages performed by Sandy McCalister 41
CHAPTER 7 RICHARD DICK MCCALISTER 42
   Marriages performed by Richard McCalister 47
   Marriages Performed by Tony B. Ratliff 48
CHAPTER 8 WESLEY MCCALISTER 49
CHAPTER 9 ISAAH (*ISIAH) MCCALISTER 50
   "Isiah's Horn" 57
CHAPTER 10 ISAAH AND MARTHA'S MCCALISTER'S CHILDREN 59
   Omina (Oma) McCalister Granville 60
   Early Bird McCalister 63
      Burnice McCalister 65
      Catherine McCalister Taylor 66
      Mable McCalister Wynn 68
   Zack McCalister 71

Vee Templeton McCalister 76
Rev. Willie McCalister 78
Willie/William McCalister *81*
Cleveland Sherman McCalister................................. *82*
Moddie D. McCalister... *84*
Elder Venoyd McCalister 86
Venoyd McCalister- Father and Son........................ 87
Charlie Kirksey McCalister *89*
Charlie T. McCalister.. 91
Richard "Uncle Dixie "Dean McCalister *92*
Larrissie McCalister.. *94*
CHAPTER 11 Meet The Henry's................................ *97*
CHAPTER 12 Family Homestead............................. *101*
Chapter 13 Family Medical History......................... *103*
CHAPTER 14 Henderson County, Texas Black Communities... *104*
CHAPTER 15 Family Reunions *118*
CHAPTER 16 Looking to the Future *123*
Final thoughts….. 129
Surname Report *130*

FOREWORD

I am a firm believer that people without family traditions, beliefs, and a continuation of the family support can lead to a crippled generation with a negative impact on future family values and relationships toward one another.

Writing a family history book is not an easy task to do when writing an illustrious heritage about the African American family. The McCalister story was not easy to research because many people in my family are not that interested in knowing what happened in the past. I felt deep in my soul, I must leave my family a book describing what life was like for our past ancestors.

I would encourage the younger generation to realize how hard it was for our fore parents to survive the atrocities of slavery in hopes that their children would have a better life than they had. This book will serve as a guideline describing our prior struggles to help the future McCalisters to continue to prosper and grow in the twenty first century.

ACKNOWLEDGEMENTS

I am grateful for those individuals that encouraged me to continue to complete this journey of finding out who I am and where I come from. I am thankful and humbled at the kindness I received from the help of my Aunt Faresa McCalister-Dawson and Aunt Zeola McCalister-Johnson, Grandmother Vee Templeton-McCalister and my Dad Rev. Willie McCalister for his C.M.E. Church history books and childhood memories. Without their assistance none of the information written would have been possible. I am very thankful that my Aunties were always patient with the incessant questioning about growing up in the McCalister family. I Love you both for never telling me to stop and those soft words encouraging me to continue my search. Thank you for that.

I thank my Uncle Joe McCalister, Aunt Carol McCalister, and Deborah Sedberry for allowing me to ride with them to all of the family funerals and various functions etc. I like to thank the late Mr. Hurley Anderson of Malakoff, Texas for sharing stories about his best friend Larrisse McCalister interesting past and pictures of the Cleveland McCalister's family. I like to say a special thanks to Mrs. Lelia Scott Henry, niece to Aunt L.B McCalister's for giving me all of her family photos and various McCalister's papers that were crucial information about our family. Thank you Raleigh Betts, the artist in the family for creating the cover for the book. You saw my vision and created a portrait of my family. I love your cousin.

Special thanks to Mrs. Willie B. Curry who helped me to know Richard McCalister and her clan. Richard was the brother of Isaah McCalister. Mrs. Curry shared everything she knew about her research and history of growing up in the Richard McCalister family. Mrs. Curry is a walking encyclopedia about our history and without her support this book would not have been possible.

To the future generation, my nephews Aaron McCalister please continue to keep the family history going for me. Christopher Frazier, Nadia Fitzpatrick, Darren Newton, Matthew and Danny Gardner I love you!

To my son, Duane Wiley always Keep God first in your life. I dedicated your life to him and asked him to always protect and keep you in his arms. He has kept his promise and I am proud of the Man you have become. I love you!

And last but not least, I thank my Uncle E.H. McCalister for teaching and showing me what family is all about. I miss you Uncle. You taught me the importance of planting seeds and watching them grow to sustain my soul. Because of you, I learned how to grow my own garden and I now enjoy watching the fruits of my labor. I love you!

CHAPTER 1 OUR BEGINNING...

Let us begin learning about our slave owners.

We come from the family of John Garrett, birth unknown, lived in Tennessee. He had a son Jacob Garrett (Charity Taylor wife) who was born about 1776 in Davidson County, Tennessee and died 1842 (Williamson County, Tennessee). Jacob moved to several locations and may have moved his family to Arkansas before he moved to the Ayish Bayou District in Texas around 1824.

Jacob served as Alcalde in 1830 and on the Permanent Council of the Mexican Government. He later settled on Attoyac River. During the years of 1830 to 1835 several municipalities which were later called counties were divided into North, south east and west divisions. Nacogdoches which is the oldest area became divided into different segments where large settlers branched out to form other communities. These locations that begin to expand were in the East Texas areas known as Nacogdoches and Bexar which was located to the West.

From Nacogdoches, the Garrets' and Ratliff families lived in several of these new formed counties. Some of those areas are San Augustine, Jasper, Liberty, Red River, Cherokee, Smith, Kaufman, and Sabine county.

Jacob had several children however his son, William Garrett was born 1808 in Davidson County, Tennessee took over much of his father's property as well as his brother Clairborn's estate at their death.

William uprooted his family and moved to the Ayish Bayou District of Texas around 1820's with 132 slaves. In 1832 he was selected as one of the committee members to select a location for a town which is currently San Augustine County, Texas. He purchased lots of land and encouraged all of his siblings to move to Texas to become prosperous cotton farmers.

Jacob and his family moved to Sabine District of Texas as shown in the 1835 census living with 5 servants and their five children whereas his son William Garrett his wife Mary Garrett and his children moved to San Augustine, Texas and was documented with their slaves in the first census of Texas in 1835.

Williams and Maria Garrett Slaves were: George, Tilman, Fanny, Moses, Lucy (wife), Maria (c), Mariah, Henry (c), Rueben, Charles, Stephen, Janke, Randall, and March.

*The Garrett's were neighbors to Frank and Minta Price whose children were: John, Mary and William. This is important because the McCalisters begin buying land. The land transaction came from the Price family in Henderson County.

William Garrett created a partnership with John Cartwright, his father in law in Sabinetown with a Cotton Warehouse. He started purchasing land with his brother in law, Matthew Cartwright. After the death of John Cartwright, William became the administrator of his father in laws estate at his death. He became a very smart and lucrative man investing in buying and selling of property. During one of his ventures he sold some land to his brother in law William D. Ratliff located on the Trinity River in Nacogdoches, later buying the property back.

William Garrett died January 12, 1884 in San Augustine County, Texas and is buried on the Garrett Plantation which is still standing. In 1962 a historical marker was placed on the plantation site.

*Family sold land to the McCalister

CHAPTER 2 THE RATLIFF'S

Evelina Garrett a sister of William Garrett was born in Tennesee on October 17, 1818. Some of the census report records her mother born in South Carolina, and her dad from Tennessee. As wedding gifts she received slaves from her parents, as well as inheriting slaves after the death of her parents. Evelina married William D. Ratliff. During the course of her marriage they both purchased slaves from her brother William Garrett. The Ratliff name was often misspelled as Ratcliff on many records and finding information about him was very difficult.

As told by other families who were enslaved and various tax records, many of the McCalister's were sold or belonged to William. D. Ratliff (W.D. Ratliff). He kept records of the number of slaves that were in his holding and listed them in his will at his death in 1862.

The earliest records of the Ratliff's were found in 1812 in the Louisiana Early Census in Feliciana Parish; no Township listed. William D Ratliff and his brother Richard Ratliff, who was a physician were born in Louisiana per census report.

His brother Dr. Richard Ratliff was married to Matilda Ballard. She had children from a previous marriage who carried the name Ballard. Richard came to Texas by way of Louisiana with his new bride and 12 slaves. The Township was Sabine District. The couple moved to Texas in 1834, and begin buying property during that time. A tax list from 1820 through 1890 in Sabine District is on file, which reflects how he and his brother William traveled closely together.

In the book called the First Census of Texas 1829 through 1836, we find in Sabine County the 1835 census has the

Ratliffs with 12 slaves listed in their home. This was one of the earliest census records of the Texas Republic. William D. Ratliff created a company of men called the San Agustine Volunteers December 1835. This group of men set off to fight in the the Texas independence from Mexico however they made it there the day ofter the Battle. Records of his trimultouse military history is documented for his military service. The company name was the San Augustine Volunteers, First Regiment, Third Brigade, No 55. This was noted in history from April 22, 1836.

According to records, a disgreement between Captain Ratliff's (Ratcliff) and his men, caused him to resign and create a new group of volunteers. For his services from 1836-1837 he was awarded a league of land in the amount of 4,000 acres according to the first class headright Certificate # 36. This property were located at Lime Stone County (Ft. Hendricks), Nacogdoches, Van Zandt known as Lockridge Hedd, and San Augustine County (Near the Attay ac. River).

In 1850, the family and their 39 slaves moved to Augustine County. During the latter part of the year, the Ratliff family moved to Henderson County, Texas. By 1850, the population of Henderson County consisted of 1,155 white persons, eighty-one slaves, and one free black. The location that the family lived was in an area called Stockard which begin as a settlement known as Caney Creek. It was about a mile or more north of its present day location. From the name of Caney Creek, the name was changed to honor Rev. Hezekiah Mitcham and Mitcham Chapel a Methodist church in 1852. The Town name had to be changed since the Texas records reflected a postal office and a town already in existence with that name. The township decided to name their area Malakoff, after a Russian town since a recent skirmish had already happen during that time frame.

Other interesting facts about Ratliff, is that he belonged to the Grand Lodge of Texas and attended the grand annual communication held at Palestine, Texas on January 19, 1857. He is listed as a Master Mason. The Ratliff family has reported 27 of their slaves and registered his marks and brands of his livestock on June 23, 1859.

His son John, registered his brand on February 4, 1860. William Ratliff family has now become a viable leading slave holder in Henderson County and is listed in the 1860's census with his slaves in the household building his community development in the Stockard Community which is located between Eustace and Athens. In 1859, twelve (12) Methodist Churches were organized and the Ratliff family members were strong supporters of the Mitcham Camp Ground Methodist Church where William Ratliff was a steward in the church. According to the history of the Methodist Church in Henderson County, his growing extended family were members there as well (Texanna Manion and her family). A second church called Walnut Creek Church was built and included Colored members. Those members were: George, Isaac, Alex, Caroline, Betne and Vinnie. All individuals were listed on Ratliff's will.

Texana's husband George D. Manion registered his brand on March 28, 1861 and noticed an error on Ratliff's name spelled as Ratcliff. On July 1, 1861 W.D. Ratliff had to correct his offical record. According to the 1860 census the total population was 4,595: 3,478 whites, 1,116 slaves, and one free black. Henderson County had over 155 slaveholders in 1860. Fincastle had the largest slave population and was the largest and wealthiest city during that time. In 1861 The Civil War had just started and Richard M. and John D. William Ratliff's sons both joined the Confederate army of Co K, 18th Texas Cavalry.

According to William D. Ratliff's military records, George Manion, his brother Rev. Alfred B. Manion, George D. Ratliff, Richard Milton Ratliff, and John D. Ratliff all served in the same company of Co K. 18th TX Calvary in 1862 during the Civil War. This association must have brought George Manion and Texana together as they later married.

William Ratliff and daughter Ann died on the same day on October 30, 1862, and the remarks listed on his tombstone states; "Covered with Glory". His Probate was filed in Henderson County, listed as W D Ratliff in Henderson Co., TX Will Book A, pg 17. The burial location in Henderson, County was in an area called the Stockard's community located in Athens, Texas, southeast of Eustace, Texas near Highway 175.

When Ratliff died in October 30, 1862, the Civil War was at the ending stages. However the family slaves were still enslaved and all of his property now belonged to his wife Evelina Ratliff. During this time many of the slaves were sold to other slave owners. William Ratliff's Estate records are listed with the names of his slaves and their value. The state of Texas and County Probate Court records dated December 1862 has Marina (sp) and her family listed as community property of W.D. and Evelina his wife. Reading prior laws, women inherited or were given slaves as wedding gifts and were allowed to keep their property; therefore the husband may also have had slaves and they were also listed as separated property. Once they purchased slaves in their marriage it became community property. Reading how these transactions occurred, split many slave families between siblings, which resulted in a tumultuous hardship that the slaves had to endure since they had no control protecting their families.

President Abraham Lincoln issued the Emancipation Proclamation on January 1, 1863, however it was not enforced in Texas until June 19, 1865 which we still celebrate as Juneteenth.

According to some of the testimony of many of Henderson County residents and newly free slaves many were very upset with Emancipation of slavery due to this happening during their harvesting season. They saw this as an insult to their prior way of living and caused undue hardship to their families because they no longer had free labor.

I do not have much information about William D. Ratliff's sons. However Texana, his daughter was listed as married to a George D. Manion, an attorney on the 1860 census. Some of the family slaves were given to Texana and her family according to the Estate records and census records for George D. Manion and Texana Ratliff. Texana's brothers John D. and Richard Milton Ratliff also were given slaves from their father. After the 1870's census, George Manion, and Texana moved to Kaufman County.

The Ratliff Family consists of:

W.D. Ratliff born in Lousiana on February 8, 1812 and died October 30, 1862 in Stockard, Henderson County, Texas.

Wife Evelina Garrett Ratliff born in Tennesee on October 17, 1818 died May 31, 1888 in Kaufman, Texas.
Children:
1. A.E. Ratliff born January 25, 1853 died July 21, 1856
2. Anna Ratliff born August 18, 1860 died October 30, 1862
3. Mary Ann Ratliff, 1836

4. John D. Ratliff, 1838
5. Texana Ratliff Manion July 14, 1845 and died May 14, 1926, (George. D. Manion)
6. Evaline (Eve) Ratliff,
7. Richard Milton Ratliff born 1843 died abt 1870 (Margaret C. Richardson July 14, 1863 Henderson County, Texas. She married *Homer Lee Parsons in 1872).
8. Betty Elizabeth Garrett Ratliff Adams born 1850, died December 3, 1878 in Kaufman, Texas. Married August 26, 1874 (Mr. Z. T. Adams)
9. Matilda Caroline Ratliff Carlisle married January 25, 1872, Kaufman, Texas (Alexander E. Carlisle)

Graves for most are located at the Ratliff cemetery in Henderson County, and Kaufman City Cemetery, Manion Plot located in Kaufman, Texas.

Texana Ratliff Picture

Evelina's children began to move to other locations including Kaufman, Texas. As she is getting older she has moved closer to her daughter Texanna who is now caring for her according to the 1880 census. Evelina Garrett Ratliff played a major roles in her children lives and even took on adopted children at the death of her daughter. Evelina died on May 31, 1888 in Kaufman and is buried in Kaufman City Cemetery. Her probate records were filed in Kaufman County, File 513, filed July 1, 1888, with her son in law, Alexander E. Carlisle as Administrator.

CHAPTER 3 SLAVE RECORDS

According to William Ratliff Estate records he has listed the names of his slaves as:

Rod, Roderick, Joe, George, Nathan (Shofner), Dave, Ben (Young), Dean, Amanda, *Elisa * FAMILY ??, *Fannie (Edwards), *Barit ,Sarah and Sam, Missouri, Robert, Henderson, Zach, Lish, Ann King and Actor, Moriah and Fanny, Eddy, Amy, Jim, and Dewitt.

The following is a list of Negroes which is listed as community property.

Simon (Shofner), Jack (Jackson) , Dick (McCalister), Dan, Tom, *Marina (McCalister), Queen (Brookins), Louisa and Rachel, Nancy, Sandy (McCalister), Caroline (Ratliff), Wesley (McCalister), and Isaah (McCalister).

Estate of W. D. Ratliff Dec'd.

The state of Texas }
County of Henderson } In S'nd County Probate court December Term 1862. To the Hon. D. S. Owen, chief justice in and for the county of Henderson. The petitioner of Emeline Ratliff who resides in Henderson County & widow of William D. Ratliff deced late of Henderson County would respectfully show unto your Honor that her said husband departed this life on the 30th day of October A. D. 1862, & that her said deceased husband left in her possession a Sealed paper represented to contain the last Will & Testament of her said husband. Petitioner represents that on the 17th day of December said sealed paper was opened by Thos. B. Greenwood & found to contain the last Will & Testament of her said dec'd husband, bearing date the ___ day of March 1860. Petitioner further states that in said Will she is appointed the Testamentary Executrix of said Will & Testament & she had no knowledge of that fact till said Sealed paper was opened on the 17th day of Decm 1862. Petitioner prays that said Will be duly probated and registered recorded in your Honors court & that she be allowed to qualify as Testamentary Executrix according to said Will & that the necessary legal notices of this application be given &c. as she will ever pray &c. Emeline Ratliff
by her atty T. B. Greenwood

" Emeline Ratliff vs. Heirs of W. D. Ratliff
Application for Probate of Will
Filed in office on this the 17th day of December A. D. 1862.
Jeff W. Thompson clk H co ct, fie, &c

The following is a list of the property of W. D. Ratliff Deceased & true & correct Inventory of all his effects both Real & Personal so far as has come to our knowledge. A list of Negroes

Names of Negroes separate property	Valuation total
Rod *Brookins	1500
Joe Brookins	1500
George Brookins	1500
Nathan Shofoner	1100
Dave	1200
Ben Young	1500
Dean	1000
Amanda	100.0
Eliza	1700
Fannie	""
Barit	""
Sarah and Sam	1000
Missouri	1000
Robert	1000
Zach	850.
Henderson	450.
Lish	1200
Ann King and Actor	1400
Moriah and Fanny	1200
Eddy King?	1200
Jim	1000
	650.

*He (William Ratliff) had numerous slaves that later changed their names to the following: Shofner, Jackson, Brookins, Mitchell, Blair, Thompson, Mays, McCalister, Pressley, and Young. Many of them had various slave owners and were often sold between Coleman, Richardson, and Williams and perhaps many others. The known last name has been italicized.

W. D. Ratliff Estate

The following is a list of negroes which is the community property in negroes & other property.

Names of Negroes Community property   value & value Total

Name	Value
Stones	200
Simon	1500
Jack	1300
Dick	800
Dan	1400
Tom	650
Morona	1300
Queen	1300
Louisa & Rachel	600
Nancy	800
Sandy	600
Caroline	600
Wesley	150
Isaiah	

The following is a list of lands & the valuation which is community property.
Names of Different tracts of land   val pr acre   value total

One Third of a Leag. of Land Lying In Lime Stone County 1476 acres Head right given to H. Hendricks Valued at $1 pr acre — $1476

One Deed for 320 acres Lying In Nacogdoches county, Valued at $1 pr acre — 320

One Deed for 320 acres Situated In Nacogdoches county Valued at $1 pr acre — 320

One Tract Situated In Henderson County W. D. Ratliff Head Right containing 4605 Valued at $3 pr acre — 13815

One Third of a Leag. Situated In Van Zandt county, known as the Lockridge Head Right 1476 acres Valued at $1 acre — 1476

1000 Acres more or less Situated In San Augustine co. on the Attay oc. River Valued at $2 pr acre — 2000

A lot of Stock & other personal effects which is community property   value total

- 80 of head — 600
- 6 Mules averaged at 100 — 50
- 2 Do " " 25 — 425
- 3 Head of Horses value — 40
- 200 Head of Stock Hogs at $2 — 10
- 7 Do Pork — 1800
- about 300 Head of Cattle $6 — 1050
- 7000 lb Pork — 2100
- 1300 Bushels corn $2 — 15
- 4300 lb Fodder 2.50 pr hd — 2520
- 72000 lb Seed cotton at $.05 — 225

The State of Texas * In the name of God, Amen.

I, William D. Ratliff, a resident citizen of the County of Henderson & State of Texas, being of sound mind and disposing memory, do by these presents make, ordain and establish this my last will and testament: that is to say that I will & bequeath to my beloved wife Emeline, all my property both real and personal to be kept by her and disposed of as follows:

First after the payment of all my just debts, including my funeral expenses I request of her to keep all of my property, both real and personal, together, and as I have already given to my beloved son, John, D. Ratliff, & my beloved daughter, Texanna Manion (formerly Texanna Ratliff) the sum of Twenty five Hundred Dollars each it is my will and desire & request that my beloved wife Eveline, do give and set apart to each one of my children as they become of age, the said sum of Twenty Five Hundred dollars: That is to say, to Milton, Matilda and Elizabeth Ratliff, all now minors; and it is my further will & desire that my beloved wife do divide equally among my children as they become of age the net proceeds of One half of each crop as it is made & sold under the following restrictions: That is to say, it is my request that she take the note of each one of my beloved children to whom she may advance any money out of the---

proceeds of my crop as is specified above with ten percent interest from date and not to become due until the maturity or marriage of my beloved daughter of youngest child Elizabeth, at which period it is my will & desire that all my property, both real and personal as well as the money advanced & the interest upon the same by my beloved wife to my said children be equally divided among them.

2nd. I desire that the Probate Court take no further notice of my estate than the Probating of this my Last will & testament and having an inventory of my estate duly returned into Court.

3rd. It is my request and desire that my wife Eveline Ratliff and she is hereby appointed my lawful executrix of this my last will and testament and that the Probate Court take no bond from her or require any bond of her, but she is hereby empowered to carry out this my last will and testament.

4th. It is my request that the Probate Court appoint Nat. P. Coleman, E. J. Thompson---------- Goodgame (Sen.) appraisers of my property, both real and personal.

All of which I declare is my last will and testament, hereby revoking all other wills, formerly made by me.

Witness my hand and seal this the ____ day of March, A. D. 1860.

W. D. Ratliff (Seal)

Signed and Acknowledged in presence of Lewis W. Moore,
            Rufus. F. Dunn
            Thos. F. Murchison.

The State of Texas) In County Probate Court, December Term,
County of Henderson) 1862.

We, Rufus F. Dunn & Thos. F. Murchison, do solemnly swear that on _____ day of March ,1860, we signed & Subscribed our names as witnesses to the instrument hereto attached at the special instance and request of William D. Ratliff, dec'd & that he signed and published said instrument in our presence as his last will and testament & that we saw the other subscribing witness, Lewis W. Moore sign & subscribed to said instrument as witness and we further swear that the said William D. Ratliff was of sound mind and disposing memory at the making and publication of said instrument, so help us God.
            Rufus F. Dunn,
            Thos. F. Murchison
Sworn to and subscribed in open Court before me, on this the 29th. December, 1862.
            Jeff E. Thompson,
            Clk. Co. Ct. He. Co.

I do solemnly swear that the writing which has been offered for probate is the last will of W. D. Ratliff so far as I know or believe and that I will well and truly perform all the duties of Executrix of---

```
-----the said Will of W. D. Ratliff, so help me God.

                                    Eveline Ratliff
    Sworn to and subscribed before me in open Court on this 29th.
    Decr. 1862.

                                    Jeff E. Thompson,
                                        Clk. Co. Ct. He. Co.
Endorsed.
    Wm. D. Ratliff-- Will.
        Filed in office for record on this 29th. day of December,
    A. D. 1862, at 12 o'clock M.
                                    Jeff E. Thompson,
                                        Clk. Co. Ct. He. Co.
    Recorded 1st. Day of January, A. D. 1863.
                                    Jeff E. Thompson,
                                        Clk. Co. Ct. He. Co.
```

When a Slave owner died, they usually left Estate records showing who their slaves were and to whom they left them with. According to records, many of the slaves that Ratliff owned were issued property by him. However, they were sold to other slave owners if debt were needed to be paid. Such is the case with Richardson, Coleman, and other leading citizens of Henderson County. Records reflect that the McCalister's, Brookin's, Coleman's, and Ratliff's slaves were sold within this group. These particular families traveled in the same location. I have found that Richardson's, Coleman's and Ratliff's all were in the San Sabine area (border of Oklahoma and Louisiana) and migrated across San Augustine, Kaufman, to Henderson County and other counties around these areas.

Rod Brookins, a former slave of W.D. Ratliff, stated that when Ratliff died, he buried him nine feet instead of six feet. When the new owner asked him why? (Coleman, was his new slave owner) he stated that he buried him deep to make sure that he would never get up. He was beaten by the new owner for this statement; however he stated it was worth it being that Ratliff was a mean man. This was told by his granddaughter Delores King when reminiscing about his slave days.

During the 1880's the remaining Ratliff family has moved to Kaufman County Texas. The census has Texana and George with a servant name Joe Chandler age 15 living in the home. In May 1888, Evalina died and is buried in the Kaufman City Cemetery instead of the Ratliff Family cemetery located in Stockard community in Henderson County, Texas.

The 1900 census has Texana, age 55 listed as a widow and running a boarding house in Kaufman on Mulberry Street. Texana was listed as living in the home with Carlisle (daughter) in 1910. In 1914 she lived on E. Moore St in Kaufman, according to the Telephone Directory. In 1920 Texana is living with Crosby, her daughter in 1920. Texana died May 14, 1926 in Kaufman. She is buried near her mother Evelina and all members of her family at the Kaufman City Cemetery.

CHAPTER 4 MARIANA'S LIFE
about 1817-unknown

The head of our family will begin with a Matriarch by the name of Mariana McCalister. Not much is known about Mariana so I will have to use all of the information from the Estate records, census report from her slave owner William D. Ratliff and daughter Caroline Ratliff McCalister-Wingfield lineage.

Researching Black family history is often very difficult since we are navigating and utilizing names from the slavery period. Since many of the slaves often carried the slave owner's last name it has created some stumbling blocks and I can only go so far with a first name.

This appears to be the case of Mariana since she was listed as community property and bought during the marriage of William Ratliff and Evelina. I have researched the Estate records of W. D. Ratliff to locate Mariana's spouse and I was unable to locate him by name. It is possible that her husband may have been sold to another family member or, he died since there is no record of who he could have been. Since Mariana belonged to Ratliff, her last name may have been the same, and perhaps she married a McCalister after she was freed. However, this raises many questions as to who actually fathered her children.

I have checked the Poll Tax records, and I was able to locate two Colored McCalister's who registered in 1867. One name was William age 59 and the other was Richard age 21. So it is possible his name was William. Richard was her second child and at the age to be drafted, so it is likely he did sign the poll tax records since he also purchased marks and brands in 1867. It is also very likely she had other children listed since Nancy is grouped with her other children on Ratliff's will. I am still trying to locate verifiable sources to prove the link association to Nancy.

Mariana was born about 1817 and died around 1881-1889 around the age of 70 or more which is a good life span for an ex-slave during that period. We find Mariana on the slave schedule census of 1850 in San Augustine Texas showing a female at the age of 35. Since the census of 1870 has her listed with her age, I have subtracted that age to find a female around the age she may have been. The slave schedule census of 1860 has a female age 45. During that time, the slaves names were not used only the slave owner name along with the ages and skin color of their property. The slave owner had to pay taxes on his property as well as give an account of his vast wealth by listing his property on earlier census report.

The Census year 1870 has Mariana or nickname "Rina" living in Henderson County, Division 3 Reel number: M593 Page number 4. According to this census her birth location is listed as Bosque, TWP, and Columbus County, North Carolina. As we find in many of the census report, much of the information about birth etc. often are incorrect as the census taker would ask neighbors about other homeowners' information if they were unable to complete their report.
Mariana is listed with her children Westly (spic), Richard, and Isaah living in Henderson County. This census also has Caroline McCalister living in the area but married to Alex Wingfield along with Sandy and his wife Hattie living next door.

Mariana was listed as a mulatto on the 1870 census, and widowed. Mulatto means that a person has a black and white ancestry. It was a common practice for the Slave

Master to rape the women slaves. She was treated horribly and her workload would have been the same as a male slave. As a slave Mariana was listed as a mulatto meaning that her mother may have been used to reproduce offspring for additional generation of slaves. Many strong women were sold as breeders during this period. If Mariana was married, the masters did not recognize slave marriages and often times split the families. There were no loyalties toward their slaves.

If a child was born to that slave woman, often times the owner sold the child because his wife would constantly see that child as a reminder of her husband infidelity. It appears that Ratliff kept his slaves together among his children. I can only imagine what life was like for a free female slave, a mother to several children trying to find a place to live in order to take care of her children. Mariana had to be strong woman who instilled pride and honor in her children because her sons began buying property and establishing family's roots to begin their new found freedom. Even though they were freed, they still lived in the same area to make sure they took care of one another.

According to the Poll Tax for property in Henderson County, Texas of 1870-1890 Mariana McCalister was granted land from the original grantee Elizabeth Washburn and was paying taxes. Mariana paid taxes up until the 1886 report. Her last names on all of these reports were spelled various ways. Here we see the names listed as; McAlister, Machalister, McCalister, McCallister and first name spelled as Mariena.

The 1880 census has Mariana "Rina"* living in the home of her son Isaah and Martha McCalister. Her age is listed as 60 with a birth location listed as Tennessee. Mariana's children Richard and Caroline are living next door to her in an area called Willow Springs, which was renamed Stockard Community.

Mariana taught her children that it was important to save money, own land and maintain the family name. She must have taught them to name their children after one another so they could find them should they be separated. The reason I state this is because all of her children named themselves after one another to remember who they were. I believe she must have done this because she was separated from her family. She had to have had a strong faith in God, because she raised two sons who became Methodist Ministers and performed various weddings beginning in 1873. These two sons were Sandy McCalister and Richard McCalister and partial listings of the weddings they performed are still recorded in the Henderson County Archive. Having ministers to perform marriages is very important in the African American community since it legitimized their relationships after emancipation.

Her children begin buying large parcels of land from prior slave owners and persons who were always in close proximity of the Ratliff families. One in particular was Sophie Price's family. The Price family children were orphaned and raised alongside the Garrett Family. William Garrett took the children in his home and raised them. So it would make sense to see Sophie Price selling property to the McCalister family. Other individuals were the Richardson Brothers, along with *Parson who sold Isaah and Wesley Brookings their first property in 1879 according to the property deed. They were each sold 200 acres of land.

According to the census records Caroline was listed as a mulatto and was the first born since her age on the census is listed at age 21. Caroline was married to Alex and her spouse was listed as a Coleman; however he changed his name to Wingfield after slavery. This would be an interesting story as to why he actually changed his name since I cannot locate any information about why it was changed.

As I was researching the family history, I noticed several similarities in the names from the Slave owner's family that also carried over to the slaves. Those names were: Charley, Richard, John, Matilda "Caroline", Zachary (Zack), and Isaah.

* Information on page 8

CHAPTER 5 CAROLINE RATLIFF MCCALISTER 1850-unknown

Caroline Ratliff McCalister was born August 1850 possibly in San Augustine Texas and died in Kaufman, Texas date unknown. According to marriage records it list Caroline name as (Ratcliff) Ratliff however her name on her children death certificate is listed as McCalister. She is listed on the census as mulatto which could mean because her mom Mariana is a mulatto her father may have been white as well (possibly William Ratliff slave master).
She is the oldest child per records from the census report. I am still trying to locate her family members who may still be living around the Kaufman, Texas area.

Caroline lineage has provided answers to many of the missing information I have had about Mariana McCalister. Caroline kept the promise and named her children after her family members. Carolina, being the oldest daughter loved her mother and it appears that she and her family stayed in Henderson County until the death of her mother.

Giving honor to her mother, she named a daughter after her. Her name is Mariana Mattie Coleman which gives me the correct spelling of her name. I am sure the other names of her children also reflect other family members and I am working to solve those puzzles. I also noticed that she named her son William, meaning that it must be the name of her father since I did find a William on the poll tax records. There are other names of interest that I will follow up on. Caroline would be the true Genealogist in the family because she left majority of our history with the namesakes of her children.

Caroline married Alex (Aless) Coleman Wingfield (A.W. Wingfield) on January 27, 1867 in Henderson County,

Texas. Marriage records states she is a free woman. Her spouse Alex's last name was listed on prior census as Coleman of which was later changed to Wingfield. According to his marriage license he is listed as freeman. I have not found out the reason behind this change other than it may have been the slave owners Nat P. Coleman's name and his parents changed their name to Wingfield. This is often the case after slavery because the slaves no longer want to be affiliated with the slave owners.

Alex Wingfield was born in January 1848 in Virginia death is unknown. He and his wife Caroline followed Texana Manion and her family as sharecroppers and farmers to Kaufman County, Texas. Caroline raised her children here and many of their off springs are still living there today. I am unable to find the death records of Caroline McCalister Wingfield as of today.

The 1870 Henderson County census has the name Alip Wingfield (sp) incorrect. The census of 1880 has her and her family living in Kaufman County, in a community called Prairieville where she and her husband were listed as sharecroppers. The family name is misspelled as Alux Wainfield instead of Alex Wingfield. The household also include Cousins: William Clark 6, Augusta Clark 3, and Mary Clark 12 as living in the family home.

The 1900 Census has Alix (52) Caroline (49) married for 32 Years per this census in Henderson County. The 1910 census has Caroline (59) born abt 1851, and Alex Wingfield (A.W.) in the household with R.L. Wren (son in law), Mamie Wren... Kaufman (Nannie Wingfield).

Based on Census reports I have listed Caroline and Alex children:

1. William Wingfield dates unknown (possibly named after her father)
2. Martha Wingfield was born in 1869 in Henderson County, Texas. Date of death unknown
   (Sister in law Martha married to Isaah)

a) Partial listings of her children are as followed: Chester Williams, James Williams, Nina Williams, Tracy Williams, Reuben Williams, Robert Williams, and Ozal L. Williams.

3. Mattie Wingfield was born in May 1873 death is unknown. She married Willie P. Scott in 1900. He was born on May 1872 in Arkansas.
a) Partial listings of her children are as followed: Dorothy Fay Scott of Kaufman, Adolphus Scott, Ruth Scott, Reldie Scott, Henry Clay Scott, Irvin Eator Scott, Wilord Scott, Annie Scott, Lonie Lee Scott, Adee Scott, Jettie Scott, A.C. Scott, Geneva Scott, Alfred D. Scott, Mosda Sott, Will Scott and Jessie Scott.

4. Mariana Wingfield was born February 8, 1877 in Henderson County, Texas and died on August 26, 1944 in Kaufman County, Texas. Her Burial is located at Flat Rock Cemetery. Mariana married Frank D. Eldridge on October 1871 and he died on January 31, 1964 in Dallas, Texas. (Her grandmother's name)

a) A partial listing of her children are as followed; John Henry Eldridge, Fred Douglass Eldridge, Callie Caledonia Nobles, Lora Belle Eldridge Scott, Genva Eldridge, Cora Naomie Eldridge Tucker,

Genon Eldrige, Mattie Liza Eldridge Scott, Mary J. Eldridge Body, and Dewey Eldridge.

5. Hattie Wingfield born in 1880 in Henderson County, Texas who married Edmond Williams. Death is unknown.
(Sister in law married to Sandy)

6. Tempie Wingfield was born on December 6, 1888 and died on August 2, 1927 in Prairieville, Texas. She married John Eldridge on December 25, 1904 in Athens, Texas.

7. Kitty Wingfield was born in February 1892 in Texas, death is unknown.

8. Mamie "Mannie" Wingfield, who was born in 1894 in Henderson County, Texas. She married Roy Lee Wren on Marcy 27, 1910. Death is unknown
a) Partial listing of her children is as followed: Cleo Wren Taylor, Gladys Wren Jordan, Cleveland Wren, Laddis Wren Jones, Geneva Wren and Leila Wren.

I don't think the names that she chose are coincidences. I think she wanted to name her children after family members who were very important in her life. Caroline may have also wanted her children to continue the tradition of knowing who their families were.

CHAPTER 6 SANDY MCCALISTER
1855-unknown

Mariana's third son was named Sandy McCalister. Not much information is known about Sandy other than he was a Methodist Minister and married families in the community. Sandy was born about 1855 in Texas according the 1870 census. Sandy age according to the 1870 census is listed as age 19 which makes his birth year at 1855. According to the 1880 census he lived outside of Athens in an area called Log Cabin outside of Athens, Texas.

I find Sandy in the Poll Tax for property in Henderson County, Texas records of 1870-1890. Sandy is paying taxes on land in 1878, 1879, 1880, 1881 and 1884. Sandy was a homeowner and acquired land to support his family. Sandy was a Minister of the Gospel and he was the first minister in the family. He began legalizing marriages in the surrounding communities for Black families. Ministers were greatly needed for the free slaves and I am sure he was outstanding in proclaiming the word of God and saving souls.

He married a Hattie Shaw on July 4, 1871 in Henderson County, by Mack Richardson, M.G. Hattie was born about 1855 in Mississippi and her mom was Katie Shaw. According to the records Sandy had two sons named Calvin and John McCalister. This branch of family members was very interesting. It seems that they set the trails of the family first migration and spelling of the McCalister name seems to have changed in majority of their locations. Once Sandy died, Hattie his widow moved to stay with her son Calvin to help raise his children. I show that Calvin and his family lived in areas called Sour Lake, and Nona Texas. This must have been a hard life for him working in a saw mill because he and his wife died at an early age. The duty of raising his children fell to his mother, Hattie Shaw McCalister.

Calvin McCalister was born about 1872 in Henderson County, Texas. Records show that Calvin married a lady by the name of Ora first. He then married Mary Haynes on January 22, 1895 in Malakoff, Texas. Mary his wife was born in 1874 in Nona, Hardin County and died about 1908 in Hardin County.

Mary Haynes family was very influential in the Hardin County communities as I was researching information about her. Date of death is unknown but most likely in Harden County, Texas.
The 1910 census has Calvan (sp) listed as head of household with his mother Hattie (58) living with him and his children.

1920 must be around the year that Calvin died, because Hattie (68) Shoulders has re-married and has his children living in Calcasieu Louisiana.
The household consisted of Lillian 20, Irene McCalister (18), Ella May (14), Viola McCalister (10).
They had several children whose names were:

1. Lillian McCalister Beverly was born on February 1896 on Nona, Texas and died November 10, 1932 in Calcasieu County due to complication of child birth. Lilian married Dilbert (Dalbert) who was born in 1901 in Lake Arthur Louisiana. He died on December 10, 1945.

2. Minnie McCalister Thomas born in March 4, 1900 in Texas and died on August 17, 1992 in Silsbee,

Hardin County, Texas. Minnie married Jerry Thomas who was born about 1894 in Texas.

3. Arrie McCalister born in 1902 in Texas and died date unknown.

4. Ella May McCalister Espree born July 23, 1905 in Texas and died in January 1981 in Lake Charles, Louisiana. She married Allen Espree.

5. Alberta McCalister born in August 12, 1911 in Texas and died on September 1978 in Lake Charles, Calcasieu, Louisiana. She married Joseph August who was born on June 16, 1912 in Louisiana. He died on March 10, 1990 in Oakland, California.

6. Irene McCalister Bias born August 10, 1905 In Kountze, Texas and died October 18, 1948 in Houston, Texas burial at Paradise Cemetery. Irene married Lawrence Bias who was born on November 20, 1902 in Louisiana. He died on September 2, 1982 in Houston, Texas.

The 1930 census has Ella M. McCalister and a Viola McCalister living in the home with James William and Patty Shoulders his mother. (She may have been Patty's sister or sister in law). Or Patty may be Hattie Shoulders with a son name James Williams. Per the Relationship of James the head of the household, Lillian is listed as his niece and her daughter is listed as a great niece. There are other children listed as well which are Dilbert Beverly who has now married Lillian Beverly McCalister her daughter Olivia Berry (2 ½), and her sisters Ella M. McCalister (17) and Viola McCalister (15). Hattie Shaw McCalister Shoulders died on November 4, 1931 at age 76 in Police Jury Ward 3, Calcasieu, Louisiana.

Now John, Sandy and Hattie second son is a mystery to me. I have found several John McCalister and I am unsure which belongs to whom. The census records have John McCalister born about 1874 in Texas. John married Louvenia (Laura) Eldridge in August 30, 1902 in Henderson County, Texas.

John married Vicie Ann Mitchell in 1922, by S.B. Barron 28, 1967, Rusk County

John Henry McCalister records were in Hardin County. Census has him born about February 5, 1886, and died June 26, 1955 at Rusk and Camp Ground Cemetery

Marriages performed by Sandy McCalister

GROOM	BRIDE	DATE
Marion Fulton	Laura Jones	January 9, 1876
Dock Hensley	Mary Derrough	September 20, 1877
Edmond Williams	Rhoda Noyes	December 24, 1877
Isaih McAllister	Martha Pinkard	December 24, 1877
Wesley Brookins	Laura Henry	December 24, 1877
Isaac Norris	Rachel Pressley	December 29, 1877
Ben Eury	Melvina Spivy	December 25, 1877
Riley Henson	Minerva Ruffin	December 29, 1877
Tom Mitchell	Angelina Hassell	March 2, 1878
Reed Brookins	Cilla Blair	March 16, 1878
George Tramell	Eliza Cogburn	May 13, 1878
George Fulton	Car. Montgomery	May 15, 1878
Jack McGruder	Carity Wood	April 14, 1880
James Williams	Lucy Boyd	August 7, 1880
Toney Ratliff	Rose Mitcham	December 11, 1880
Frank Carroll	Eliza Kelly	December 22, 1880
Berry Sims	Louisa Wiley	August 17, 1882
Ben Young	Mary Jane Brookins	November 15, 1883
Ely Davis	Lena Fulton	December 25, 1883
Press Brown	Martha Fulton	December 20, 1883

CHAPTER 7 RICHARD DICK MCCALISTER
April 1849-Sept 20, 1932

Richard "Dick" McCalister would be her second child, listed as age 17 in the 1870 census. His death certificate state he was born about April 1849 in San Augustine County, Texas and died on September 20, 1932 in Malakoff, Texas. Richard D. McCalister was buried at Antioch Cemetery.

Richard was a hard worker and a productive provider for his family. At an early age he began to build his family empire. It appears that he took over the family affairs and commence to buying land so that his family would have a place to live and produce livestock as well as growing crop to sustain the family needs. He became a prosperous farmer and at an early age he also applied for his own Patent mark and brand of cattle on February 19, 1869 page 264. Name listed was spelled McAlester on this record. Richard must have felt the responsibility of being the head of his mom's Mariana household.

He quickly made the McCalister name a leader in the community. He registered to vote according to the Black Voters Registration List dated July 29, 1867 page 59. Richard became a minister of the Gospel and began marrying families in Henderson County, Texas. Richard "Dick" name on deed, purchased large quantities of land on the waters of Cany (sp) Creek 5 ½ miles North 35 degrees West of Athens beginning at the N.E. Corner of a Survey which is now known as the Saint Paul community from A,H, Green on the 17th day of June 1872. In the year of 1871 Dick (name as shown on land records) is paying Poll Tax for property in Henderson County, Texas according to the 1870-1890 Tax Records. He was paying taxes to the original grantee of Graham for 60 acres. Richard McAlister (sp) sold this land to Allen Abbey (who was also another black land owner) Grantee. Date of instrument, June 17, 1872 with a number of 63 Acres dated July 23, 1872, considerations of property 80.00, Book Q, page 261. Dick was the name he is often referred to during the early 1870's, 1880's and 1890's.

In 1874 Richard is paying taxes on land owned by Graham 60 acres. In 1879 He is paying taxes on land owned by the original grantee to Jane Irvine about 160 acres valued at $550.00.

In 1880 Richard owns 40 hogs and a few cows that he is paying taxes for. Richard is still paying taxes on all of his property and it seems he acreages that he purchased has decreased to 132 ½ to Jane Irvine because a supplement was added on page 72-73.

On November 1, 1892 M.E. Eustace and her husband W.T. Eustace sold 132 ½ land situated in Henderson County, Texas part of the Jane Irvin League to Jno Richardson. Deed transferred as of October 15, 1910.

Richard has also purchased other property in the St. Paul community area and this property is still with Richard McCalister's family and many of his descendants are still living there today (2014).

Richard Dick was a strong believer in education, and donated several acres of land for schools to be built in Saint Paul community which was known as Caney City. The schools were still used to educate the African American community until the schools became integrated in Henderson County, Texas. St. Paul Training School was located in this community and many family members attended the school. At one time talk to reopen the school as training was on the towns agenda, however due to lack of funding etc. the school was torn down.

Richard encouraged and instilled education and hardworking values in his children because he wanted them to become prosperous in every stage of their lives. During that time, Richard is listed as a Minister of the Gospel performing marriages in Henderson County, in the 1873-1874 records.

He married Mariah Young William on October 25, 1868 in Henderson County, Texas License found in Vol. 1, page 28, of 1868. Mariah had a son and daughter whom Richard raised named Toney Ratliff and a daughter name Anna Young Ratliff. Tony followed in his stepfathers footsteps and became a Minister of the Gospel.
Richard was a Minister of law and performed several marriages in Henderson County. He performed the marriage of his daughter Nellie McCalister to E. Williams.

Children of Richard and Mariah Young are:
1. Antonio (Toney) B. Ratcliff was born November 15, 1863 in Texas. He died on February 24, 1937 in Corsicana, Texas. Burial location is Woodland Cemetery. Tony (his nickname) was Mariah William Young McCalister first born son. His father was named Bill Ratcliff. Antonio was a carpenter by trade according to his death certificate. He married Amanda Brookins and they had a daughter named Mable Ratcliff Caldwell born June 17, 1903 and died February 28, 1971 in Athens, Texas. He then married Rosa Mitchell Cason on December 11. 1880. Rosa was born May 1870 in Corsicana and

died on August 20, 1911 in Corsicana, Texas. Children: Tennessee, E.F., Omis, Ada,

2. Anna Ratliff - I have no information on her.

3. Lillie was born on June 1886. She married Henry Davis on August 24, 1901 and married Monroe Johnson on June 12, 1915.

4. Isaiah Hillory (Nicknames: I.H. and Bud) was born on October 10, 1873 in Malakoff, Texas and died on May 19, 1949 in Malakoff, Texas. Burial location is Antioch Cemetery. I.H. married Katie Brown who was born in November 17, 1894. He later married Eddie Roberson Brookins on October 30, 1902 in Athens, Texas. Death is unknown. Isaiah was a school trustee and also donated land for a school. Mrs. Willie B. Curry and other family members remember his favorite saying was "Make Hay while the sun is shining".

Eddie Roberson

Alzada was born February 9, 1876 in Texas and died on December 4, 1934 in Malakoff, Texas. Burial location is at Antioch Cemetery. Alzada married Tom Wiley on October 13, 1895. He was born February 1876 and died 1920.

5. Nellie was born on April 1879 in Malakoff, Texas and died on February 13, 1952 in Malakoff, Texas. Nellie married Ennis Williams on October 30, 1897 in Henderson County.

6. John Mack "Hoxie" was born on

February 20, 1881 in Dawson, Texas and died on June 30, 1928 in Dawson, Texas. He married Louvenia on August 30, 1902, married Savannah,

7. Edith "Ettie" was born on August 1882 in Malakoff, Texas died date unknown. She married Jerry Wiley date unknown.

8. America was born on January 28, 1892 in Malakoff, Texas and died July 28, 1982 in Malakoff, Texas. America had no children.

R. D. McCalister (McAllister) is listed as a Pioneer of Henderson County. His name is listed in the History of Henderson County Texas: recording names of early pioneers, their struggles and handicaps, conditions and appearance from 1865-1875. According to the 1900 census, Richard McCalister is now age 49, and states that his father was born in Maryland and his mom was born in Tennessee.

Marriages performed by Richard McCalister

GROOM	BRIDE	DATE
Thomas Harris	Sarah Larue	May 17, 1873
Wesley Brookins	Rachel Mayes	July 20, 1873
Anderson Thorn	Percilla Carter	July 11, 1873
Jordan Brookins	Lizette Brookins	December 28, 1873
Dennis Palmer	Mary Ellen Ellick	December 31, 1873
Columbus Worley	Lucy Ann Hines	December 9, 1874
Henry Durrough	Annie Dykes	August 22, 1875
Peter Benson	Lucy Derden	February 6, 1876
B.N. Hardin	Ann Davis	November 30, 1884
Wm. Davis	L. A. Barlow	November 25, 1884
Fayette Adams	Lucetta Young	December 3, 1884
Tom Blair	Queen Thompson	June 11, 1885
Charlie Shaw	Mary J. Thomas	February 13, 1886
Robert Martin	Julie Thompson	August 12, 1886
Ed Jones	Mary Spivy	March 26, 1887
Preston Thompson	Manda Moore	January 23, 1890
Roderick Brookins	Nancy Ellen Martin	November 9, 1890
Frank Blair	E.M. Dixon	December 18, 1890
Sam Rushing	Arlevia Brookins	January 8, 1891
Abe Wilson	Nancy Martin	April 17, 1892
D. D. Williams	Bulah Lee Thompson	February 10, 1894
Tom Wiley	Alzada McAllister	October 13, 1895
Will Griffin	Sallie Ann Young	October 12, 1895
Henry Cook	Roxana Young	April 25, 1895
Will Richardson	Annie Shaftner	July 14, 1897
Dewitt Young	Mollie Blair	July 27, 1897

Marriages Performed by Tony B. Ratliff

George Prock	Evaline Brookins	Jan 6,1896
Isaiah McAlister	Katie Brown	Nov. 17,1894
George Bobb	Manda Brookins	July 19,1894
William Brown	Ella Johnson	Mar 18,1894
John Murphy	Mary Jackson	Aug 11,1893
Al Mitchell	Ada Kemelian	Dec. 20,1891
Lewis Thompson	Emma Terell	Apr. 26,1890
Willie Brown	Laura Brookins	Dec. 24,1889
Peter Scruggs	Adella Brookins	Dec. 24,1889
Charley Brown	Lizzie Franklin	Jan 23,1888
Geo. W. Tramel	Ellen Brown	Jul. 7,1887

CHAPTER 8 WESLEY MCCALISTER
1855-unknown

Wesley McCalister would be the fifth child and the baby of the family since he is listed as age 15. I have no information on a Wesley McCalister other than what has been listed on the Census reports. It is possible that Wesley may have died at an early age. I am still researching for information on him.

Other possibilities are that his name may have been Willie, William or John Wesley.

CHAPTER 9 ISAAH (*ISIAH) MCCALISTER
February 1852- September 25, 1907
Martha McCalister
March 3, 1856- February 15, 1925

Isaah McCalister was the fourth child born to Mariana. Isaah was a very strong and independent man whose family values must have been instilled in him from his mother. He appeared to have been a strong Christian, and a family man. He knew after slavery was abolished that he must create a way to provide for his mother and his family. I can only imagine what life was like in Henderson County, after slavery was abolished. It must have been hard deciding how he and his brothers and sister were going to provide for themselves and their family.

When checking the census records, I know that he could write since he was able to sign all of his deeds transaction so he must have been educated. I find Isaah in the 1870's census, living with his mother Mariana along with brothers Sandy, Westley, Richard. I later find him in the 1880's census now married to Martha Pinkard McCalister, marriage performed by his brother Sandy McCalister on December 25, 1877. He was listed as farmer in the 1880 census and it showed that he had purchased some property.

Isaah purchased several acres of land. His first transaction was 80 acres from the original owner Sophia Price* dated 26th day of February 1879 book 36 page 346. The land was paid off in 1886 and J.J. Richardson and Brothers would issue the deed over to Isaah on the date of the last note of October 1, 1889. Sophia Price also sold 160 acres over to Wesley Brookings and 160 acres over to Isaah McCalister on October 25, 1886.

Isaah and Martha McCalister sold 26 acres of land located on lot number 4, to W.C. Smith and W. J. Evans on September 16, 1896 book 38, and page 79.
Isaah also purchased 53.88 acres of land on November 1, 1900 of the William Ligon survey situated 3 ½ miles southwest of the town Malakoff and known as lot XII owned by John D. Patterson (living in Ontario County, New York) and B.J. Williams (Navarro County, Texas). The amount of sales was for $169.40 today's amount of $18,179.92. This information is located on Volume 44, page 238. This land proved to be a wealth of resources in the Malakoff, Texas community. This property was mismanaged and neglected and stolen from the family.

This same land was under probate when J. F. Williams and John D. Patterson died. Independent executors of the will were W. W. Patterson and Thomas W. Patterson. Moddie, Charlie, Richard (Dixie), and Larrisie McCalister had to pay a sum of $273.55 for the reminder of the 40 acres of land located on volume 44, page 44 of the deed records of Henderson County, Texas. Date of deed is December 5, 1911.

Rev. Willie McCalister and Dr. Joe McCalister took this family to court and lost due to squatter's right and failure to pay taxes on the land. A wealthy Doctor family has taken over the property and has had it for years. Per the courts, since the land did belong to the McCalister family they can only retain the mineral rights to the property. Vee McCalister was getting a very small check from the company that is still producing oil on the property today.

Isaah was a hard worker had a strong business sense, and instilled good work ethics with his sons because they all purchased and maintained their property. Issah McCalister is listed on the 1890 Tax Rolls, Henderson County, Texas Resident Owner Renditions. He is paying for 80 acres of land surveyed by Peter Tumlinson.

He must have entrenched in his children the importance of entrepreneurship and owning things in your name, since the McCalister's went about purchasing and using their money to better future generations. Isaah died from cancer on September 25, 1907. He had worked all his life to provide and care for his mother, wife and children. He had a dream that he surely wanted his sons and daughter to continue to prosper for their children and the future generation.

As a precaution to protecting his family, he created a will deeding his 80 acres over to his wife and heirs. Each of his children received a copy of the land along with their plots. This is located in Volume 36 on page 346 on the Deed Records and Volume 136 page 51.

The lots were as recorded:
Lot number 1 Cleveland Sherman McCalister and Rosa McCalister
Lot number 2 Larrisse McCalister and Lillian McCalister
Lot number 3 R.D. McCalister and Jewell McCalister
Lot number 4 Zack McCalister
Lot number 5 Charlie McCalister and Emma McCalister
Lot number 6 M.D. McCalister and Savannah McCalister
Lot number 7 Early McCalister and wife A.B. McCalister

Lot number 8 Heirs of Oma McCalister Granville Della Granville, Isaah Granville, George McDonald, Resa Johnson, Will Johnson, Beatrice McDonald

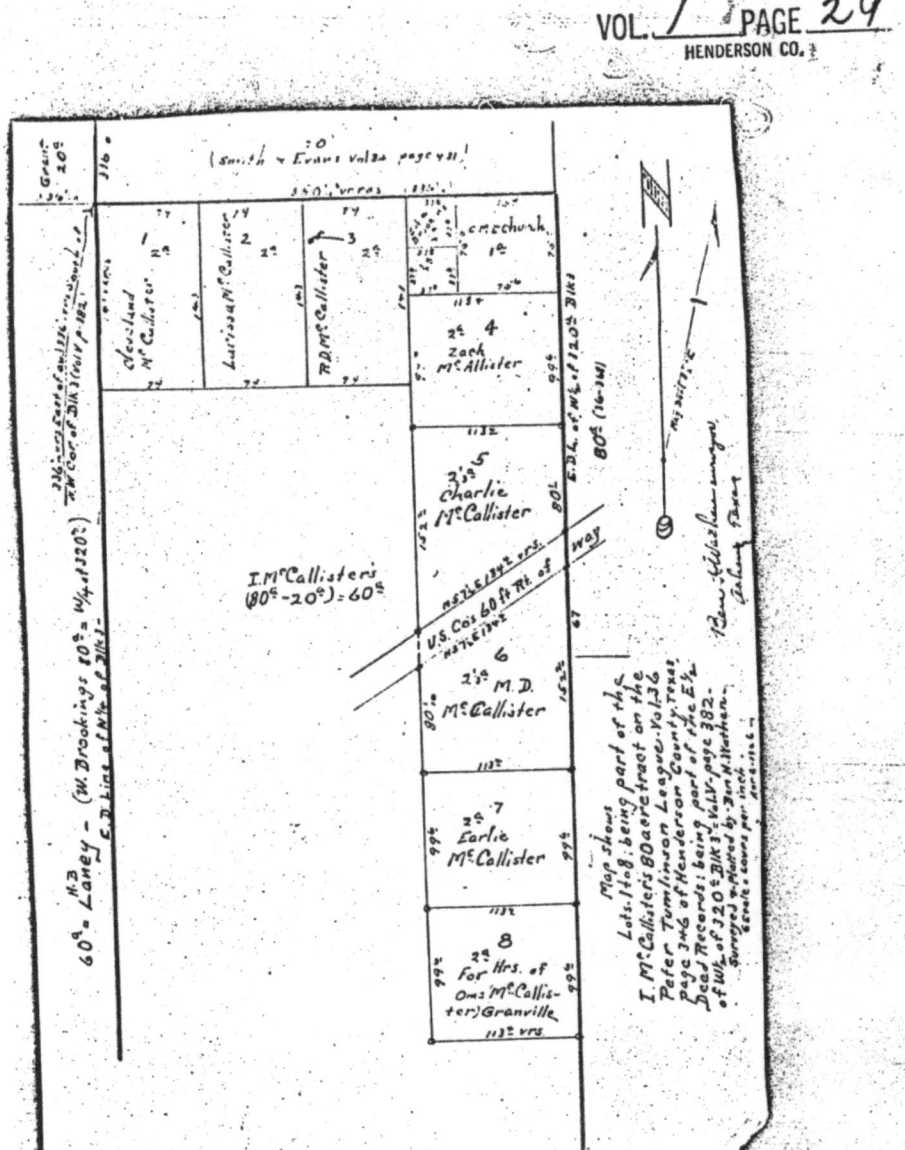

| | | (Wife Jewell McCalister) |
| | | Bros & Sisters |

- 1/8 — Larissa McCalister
  et ux Lillian

- 1/8 — OMA McC. Granville D
  et vir Dallas Granville D
  - Beatrice Granville McDonald
    et vir George
  - Iziah Granville
  - Resa Granville Johnson
    et vir Hubbard
  - Lather Granville - D
    et ux Idella - D
    - Lawrence Granv
    - Ola Mae Granville
      et vir Louis
    - Wilmer Granville
      et ux Neeni ± (S
    - Coral Granville

- 1/8 — Early McCalister D
  et ux Lizzie Bell
  - Myrtle McC. Butler
    et vir Mark
  - Burnice McC
    et ux Almeta
  - Mabel McC Wynn
    et vir Spiegeon
  - Fred McC - single
  - Esenk McC -
  - Early Hugh McC - single
  - Ed McC - single
  - Katherine McC. Taylor
    et vir Leon

- 1/8 — C.S. McCalister
  et ux Rosie

- 1/8 — R.D. McCalister D
  et ux Jewel -

  Survivors -
  Wife Jewell McCalister
  Bros & Sisters
  Nieces & Nephews

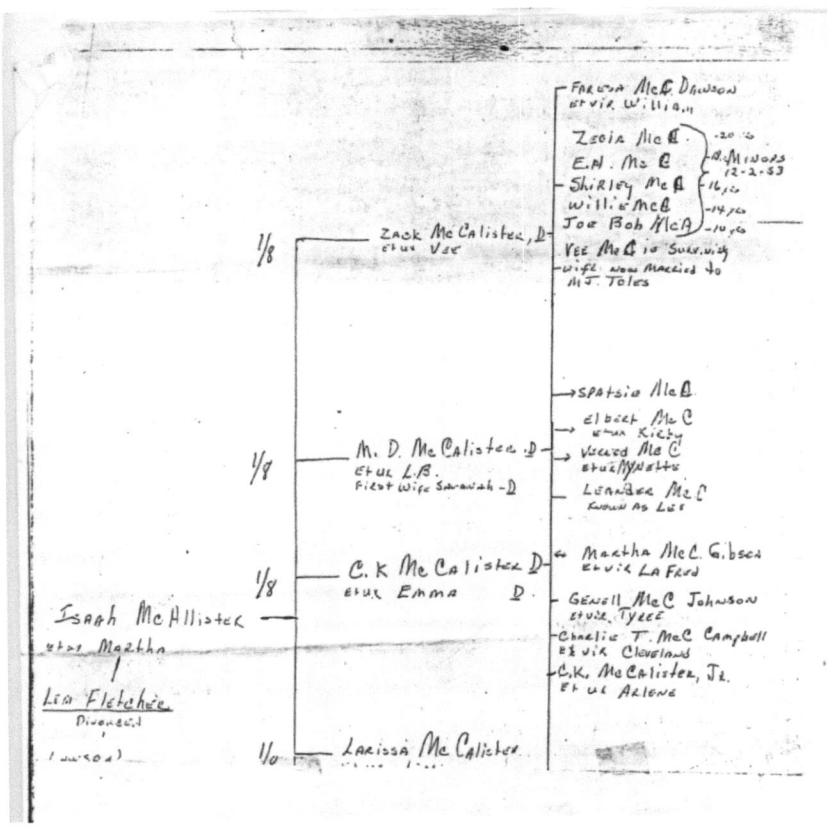

After his death, Martha was very business savvy and managed the family's ownership of lots of acres of land, and even provided land easements for the railroad to come through. Deed records of all of her accomplishments are documented in Court Records. Martha also allowed oil companies to drill on the land and received royalties from these transactions.

Martha also had a will in place to ensure that her children knew where their property was located. She split up the 80 acres of land and had plots designated to each of her living children or heirs on June 14, 1926. This paperwork was given to each son and they passed the land over to their children. Today, the only person who has an original copy is in the possession of Charlie T. McCalister Campbell's family.

The information has the names of all the heirs. This was very vital since it gave me the names of their spouses and their children. From this document, I was able to also verify the marriages of Martha McCalister.

As the brothers set their goals on property in other counties or state, they sold their land to Cleveland McCalister or one of their other brothers. During their lifetime, the brothers held on to their property for their children or leased the property to other settlers in the Malakoff, Texas area.

*Isaah name has many variations used throughout all of his land transactions, deeds and census records. Family records have his name listed as Isaah which is the traditional spelling. I am going to use what the records reflect as Isaah.

"Isiah's Horn"
"This horn is old and it's worn.
"It belonged to my dad before I was born"

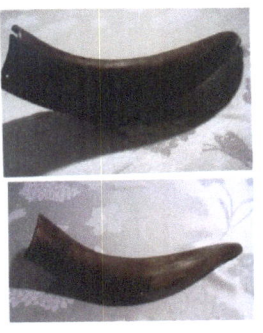

This is the story of Isiah's horn as remembered by his son, Charley Kirk McCalister and his granddaughter, Charlie Theresa McCalister Campbell.

"Memories of my dad by Charlie Kirks"... When I was a very young boy, Pa (Isiah) and his friends went hunting often. Pa owned several hound dogs. On days when they were planning a hunting trip, Isiah would blow the horn to alert the dogs. At the sound of the horn, all the dogs would stand and howl. He always carried the horn on trips that led to dense and wooded areas. If they got lost he would blow the horn and neighbors would go out and search for them.

Note: Charley called his parents Ma and Pa.
"As remembered by Charlie T" Where did Isiah get this horn? Did his dad leave it to him? Is this horn of a buffalo or wild ox that roamed this country long ago? I do not have answers for these questions.

Years later when I was a little girl, it was my job to blow the horn at 12 noon for the field hands to come to dinner. I was too young to pick cotton or tell time. My mother told me that when both clock hands were on the 12 to blow the horn. If a family member became seriously ill or some disaster occurred, we could always get help immediately by blowing the horn. Remember we had no telephones at that time. I never knew grandpa Isiah; I believe that he was a very smart business man. He enjoyed hunting and fishing. This horn was very special to Charley, Emma and their children. May it be passed to future generations of

McCalister family for many years. May it bring joy to all when they think of Isiah, Martha and years gone by. Proud to be their granddaughter, Charlie T. McCalister Campbell

Written on October 10, 2010

CHAPTER 10 ISAAH AND MARTHA'S MCCALISTER'S CHILDREN

Larrissie

Oma or Omina

Cleveland

Early

Zack

Moddie

Charlie

Willie or Richard

Omina (Oma) McCalister Granville
January 1878 - July 25, 1908

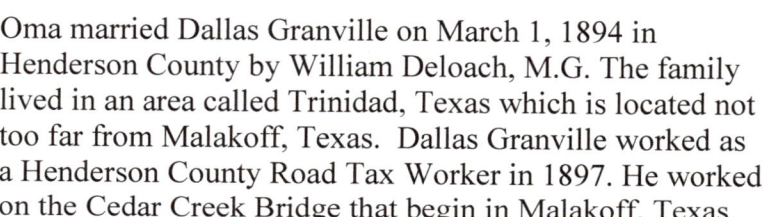

Oma McCalister Granville was born in 1878 in Malakoff, Texas to Martha McCalister. She was the eldest and only daughter of the couple's ten children. Oma was named after Martha's mother who was named Oma Henry.

Oma married Dallas Granville on March 1, 1894 in Henderson County by William Deloach, M.G. The family lived in an area called Trinidad, Texas which is located not too far from Malakoff, Texas. Dallas Granville worked as a Henderson County Road Tax Worker in 1897. He worked on the Cedar Creek Bridge that begin in Malakoff, Texas.

I asked my grandmother, Vee McCalister about the history of Oma. She states she has very little information about Oma. However, Mr. Zack use to tell her that Oma was killed by her husband Dallas Granville when she was out in the field washing clothes. She stated that Dallas asked to borrow a gun from one of her brothers to hunt squirrels; he shot her three times, and left the body in the field. When her parents sent out a search party to find her, she was found blistered and burned in the hot sun. This news shook the community and made the local news in the Athens weekly Review. Dallas was prosecuted according to the article, and was imprisoned in Fort Bend in 1910.

Athens Weekly Review August 9, 1928
20 YEARS AGO Athens Weekly Review

Items from the Review files of July 30, 1908
Dallas Granville, a Negro in the Malakoff-Trinidad country, killed his wife Saturday by shooting her three times. County Attorney Bishop, John A. Mobley, E.P. Miller and Sherriff John W. Wood went to Malakoff Thursday to attend the examining trial of Dallas Granville who was charged with murdering his wife.

Dallas was convicted and imprisoned on October 17, 1908. It continues to show him still in prison in the 1910 census at the 4th Justice prescient in Fort Bend, Texas. Dallas Granville was released from prison on January 28, 1913. His stay in prison was not easy and he had many health issues once he was released. Martha McCalister his mother in law saw him walking on the highway felt sorry for him and picked him up in her wagon. She had forgiven him for killing her only daughter.

The 1920 census has Dallas Granville married to Callie Jackson Sloan. Dallas marries Callie on June 12, 1915, Volume 9 page 189.
Other information unknown

During the early 1900, the Granville family owned large tracts of land in the area called Jackson Lake. Several of them lived in Trinidad as well. Some of the family members are buried at Trinidad Cemetery and Antioch Cemetery.

Children of Oma and Dallas Granville are:
1. Beatrice Granville McDonald July 7, 1896 in Malakoff, Texas and died on September 25, 1962 in

Brownwood, Texas. She married George McDonald.
2. Isaiah Granville born 1902 in Malakoff, Texas and died on September 6, 1958 in Dayton, Ohio.
3. Resa Granville Johnson born July 7, 1903 in Malakoff, Texas and died on January 19, 1978. Herbert Wilbert Johnson.
4. Ruther Granville born September 7, 1900 in Malakoff, Texas and died date unknown. Marriages Harriett Blair on November 18, 1918 and Idella Green on January 5, 1921.

Isiah

Resa

Early Bird McCalister
January 20, 1882 – January 4, 1946

Early Bird McCalister, second child of Martha and Isaah McCalister was born in Malakoff, Texas. He attended Texas College in Tyler Texas, married and reared a family of eight children. His first wife was the late Annie Hoard McCalister of whom he married December 21, 1902 in Henderson County, Texas. From this Union three lovely children were born:
1. Mrs. Myrtle McCalister Butler
2. Mr. Burnice McCalister
3. Mrs. Mable McCalister Wynn

Annie Hoard McCalister died while their youngest child, Mable was still an infant. Sometime later, Mr. Early married Allie Bell Graves on November 19, 1911 in Henderson County, Texas. God blessed them with four healthy sons and a beautiful baby daughter. The children are as follows:
4. Mr. Fred McCalister
5. Mr. Oscar McCalister
6. Mr. Early Hugh McCalister
7. Mr. Edd McCalister
8. Mrs. Catherine McCalister Taylor

Early McCalister was prepared to teach school, but to his dismay, he found that he was unable to provide for his family, with the salary paid. He then decided to continue farming, saving his money, and investing in real estate. His first investment was the purchasing of two hundred (200) acres of land in Oakwood. Later he sold some acres and purchased a large parcel of land in a sub-division of Oakwood called Shiloh and an area called The River Bend. There the families were share croppers producing cotton. Early McCalister also purchased land in the St. Paul community.

Mr. Early was a Christian Man, blessed abundantly with many talents, gifts and graces. He was an entrepreneur of the highest magnitude, with the ability and desire to succeed. He worked hard and made wise investments which in time allowed him to prosper. He was also a caring and sharing person, who openly expressed concern for the well-being of others. He loved and helped many people and was loved in return by his family, friends and acquaintances. According to the Malakoff newspaper, the first bale of cotton ginned at the Malakoff Gin was that of Early McCalister weighing 449 pounds and was purchased by Peel Dodson at .29cent per pound. The bale, together with the seed netted the owner a total of $154.71.

One day, while sitting on the front porch, Grandpa shared a concept with me that I think he would want me to share with you. When I was five years old, he asked me a question that I haven't forgotten. "What would you do with a calf, if I gave one to you?" "I replied, "I would kill it and eat it", he said, "NO, you should wait until the calf becomes a cow, and has other calves, then you kill one of the calves and eat it. "He expounded on the concept thoroughly. I would like to paraphrase this concept for the younger descendants. "Do not spend (kill) all of your money (calves). Save and/or invest some of your money and wait for it to mature and produce other money (calves)".

Early McCalister was killed by a horrible violent Two F-4 tornado that hit that area in January 4, 1946 destroying much of the community in East Texas. Its destruction killed 28, injured 310 and caused up to $2.1 million worth of damage. This storm was very unusual, especially when it hit the same areas. Early's body was found in a tree.

Burnice McCalister

Son to Early McCalister was born in March 9, 1906-May 25, 1986. He married Almeta Butler in December 6, 1931. Almeta Butler was born on August 26, 1916- July 13, 1985. Burnice graduated from H.S and went to College (unknown high school and college) and worked in the Glass Factor, farmed in Palestine, Texas and helped to build the Golden Gate Bridge in San Francisco, California.
Burnice attended an AME Methodist Church in Palestine, Texas.

Burnice and Almeta had seven lovely children. The children names are:
Annie Mae deceased 1967(Albert Edwards)-5 children; Ervin, Delois, Donald Ray, Gwen and Karen
Bernice -2 children; Leonard Whitman Jr, Stanley Whitman
 Cecil deceased 1978(Mary Lois) -4-children; Ronald Earl, Lisa, Mechela, Kay
 Willie -5 children; Jackie, Greg, Willie Jr, Detra, Anthony
Elvin (Marie)-2 children; Mickey, Elvin Jr
Vannoy, deceased 2004 (Stella) -7children; Howard, Rosalyn, DoResha, Sylvia, Vannoy Jr., Vanetta, Venitra
 Robert, -11children; Ray, Derek, Cedrick, Kendra, Crystal, Terry, Dell, Darrell, Shemaka, Robert Jr., Jermaine

Memories of Burnice…..
"He told his son's that since he moved to OKC, he quit smoking and drinking, but he thought that he would live longer if he had not stopped" –Bernice
"He told me that I looked better than he though since he had cataract surgery! He had not seen me in 10 years" – Bernice
"Daddy took all us boys to bail cotton and made a deal with the cotton field owner that if we finished by noon on that Saturday, he would pay him $50 and they could go shopping in town. So they finished by 11:30 and the man

paid them but ran them off, because he did not expect us to finish by that time" –Robert

Catherine McCalister Taylor
April 25, 1921 – July 20, 2004
After already having two lovely girls and five fine boys in their immediate family, Early and Allie Bell McCalister were just as excited to add another beautiful baby girl, our Aunt Catherine. Catherine was born on April 25, 1921 in Leon County city of Oakwood, Texas. At the age of four, she, her brothers Oscar, Fred, Early Hugh and Ed attended the same elementary school, Magnolia in Oakwood, from first to the eighth grade. Their cousins Charlie T. Would join them in the fifth grade. Catherine's two sisters Myrtle and Mable were attending another school. Miss Underwood was Aunt Catherine's first grade teacher.

After being promoted to the ninth grade from Magnolia Elementary School, Catherine, her siblings, and cousin enrolled in St. Paul High School there in Oakwood. At St. Paul, Aunt Catherine enjoyed acting in school plays, portraying various characters. Aunt Catherine was extremely popular, for all the students knew and liked her. Following in her father's footsteps, Catherine chose to matriculate at his alma mater, Texas College in Tyler, Texas along with her dear cousin Charlie T. Catherine majored in economics and minored in sociology. She truly enjoyed her college years. After receiving her degree, Catherine wanted to teach elementary school. She received a job offer in Sea Grave, Texas near New Mexico, which she accepted.

Unfortunately, Catherine did not enjoy teaching children in elementary school as much as she had anticipated, so after one year, she made a decision to reside in Galveston where her sister Myrtle and her husband Mark lived. This was also the city where her cousin Charlie T. resided with her husband Cleveland.

Later on Catherine's second oldest sister Mable and her husband Spergon came to live in Galveston.

After being single for several years, Catherine met a handsome manager/cook who was employed by a small café on 29th and Market Street. This gentleman was Leon Taylor who Catherine later fell in love with and married while in her thirties. Leon was a widower with four adult children: Leon Jr., Robert, Ruth, and Mary Kathryn.

On July 24, 1959 at St. Mary's Hospital a precious baby boy, Walter Earl Taylor was born to this happy couple. Catherine and Leon were ecstatic and excited about their bundle of joy. Walter grew and became the center of their lives. They gave him all of their attention and inundated him with love.

After being married for nine years, one day in 1961 Uncle Leon was crossing the street when he was suddenly hit by an automobile. The accident was a tragedy and Uncle Leon died within two weeks.

After the death of Uncle Leon, Aunt Catherine raised Walter Earl by herself. Aunt Catherine and Walter worshipped faithfully at Shiloh A.M.E. Church, and when she was too sick to attend she sent Walter alone. Aunt Catherine was a very strong proponent of education. Walter knew the first order of business immediately after school was homework. As a Reward for his good behavior and academic work, Aunt Catherine would cook his favorite food. When Walter was very young, Aunt Catherine taught Walter how to cook, shop, and pay their bills. Walter was always very neat and clean. He was one of the first African American students to attend Ball High School after it became integrated. After graduation from Ball High School, Walter attended Prairie View College in Prairie View, Texas.

Aunt Catherine helped all of her nieces and nephews at some point in her life. For example, she has often taken us to the physician for illness or physical examinations while our mother worked. She assisted our mother in other endeavors such as making our clothes and cooking our meals for us when mother was very ill. For Christmas, she and Aunt Myrtle would sometimes give us gifts. Other nieces and nephews have also received help in the form of money, clothing and school supplies. Aunt Catherine would often help both of her sisters with baking, cooking, and church work. She helped many people with their income taxes. In general, Aunt Cat was excellent about reaching out to help her immediate family and friends, as well as helping anyone who was in need. Aunt Catherine was living the way that Jesus has taught us in the scriptures. She still loved to read the Bible and pray. Aunt Catherine is the last and youngest member of the Early McCalister Family. Aunt Catherine is blessed to have her son Walter, Niece Hazel, nephew Leon and Cousin Charlie T and other relatives to regularly visit and call her.
Catherine is the last and youngest member of Early McCalister Family.

July 16-18 2004 Reunion
This bio was written by the Early McCalister Family members for the July Reunion

Mable McCalister Wynn

Mable McCalister was born on June 29, 1910 in Galveston, Texas and died March 3, 2003 in San Francisco, California. Mable married Spergon Wynn, Sr. and had the following children: Mrs. Opal Wynn McCoy, Mrs. Hazel Jean Wynn Henderson, Mrs. Barbara Elaine Wynn Thomas, Mr. Spergon Wynn, Jr, and Mr. Charles Edward Wynn.

Train up a child in the way he should go; and when he is old he will not depart from it. Proverbs 22:6

Mother, we honor you for your training. You taught us to: always tell the truth, obey your parents, love and respect each other and do not fight. "If you don't respect your sister or brother, neither will your friends." Do unto others as you would have them do unto you. Study hard. Graduate from High School and College. Be on time and always work hard. "Since you have to work, you need to get the highest pay for each hour. It is the same hour! You decide what you want to be paid and prepare yourself to receive it." SAVE and INVEST YOUR MONEY!!! Attend Sunday school and Church; accept Christ as your Personal Savior. Read and Study the Bible. To be a lifelong learner; we learned to be LIFT LONG LEARNERS from your example, of continuing to read, travel and study until your eyesight became impaired. God Bless you, Sweet Angel Mother, for training us in the way we should go. Your training has kept us safe, alive and well. We continue to live by the tenants you taught us long ago.

Mother, we honor you for your courage. One night long ago, when Daddy was gone to Galveston to seek employment, someone tried to break into our house. When the burglar flashed a bright light inside our house, it frightened me. The next thing I knew, you were up in the window looking like you wanted to ring his neck. That gave me the courage to get in the window also because I was no longer afraid.

Mother, we honor you for your sacrifices. You sometimes worked two jobs so you could buy fabric to make Easter dresses and put those suits on lay-a-way. Mother we honor your strength it took to deny you own needs for the needs of your children. We love you Mother, because you sacrificed your life to make a better life for us. You had the

physical strength to work hard and yet come home and take care of us, nurture and teach us. You were always encouraging us to be the best that we could be.
Mother, we honor you for your expertise. You were an excellent homemaker. We remember those delicious meals, especially chicken every Sunday after church. Christmas was the greatest time of the year; new clothes, apples, oranges, peppermint candy and possibly a toy or two for each of us. We had chicken on Christmas but you added dressing to make it special. We cannot recall seeing your new Christmas or Easter dress, but you went to church anyway and Praise the Lord!

We honor, praise, adore, and thank you for the numerous sacrifices you made on our behalf.

Zack McCalister
January 28, 1884- June 25, 1945

Zack McCalister was born in Malakoff, Texas, third child to the parents of Martha and Isaah McCalister. Zack had very little schooling because he and his brothers had to work as farmers to maintain their family farm. They also worked to pay off the property debts when their father died on January 1907. Their father, Isaah had set the standards and instilled in his children that they must learn to manage their money, purchase property and maintain and create sources of income to feed their families. Zack owned a lot of land that he farmed along with his brothers Larrissie, and Richard McCalister (according to farm deed and records).

Zack was very business oriented and he was a great mathematician. He knew how to manage his property and livestock. According to many of the deed records, Zack sold several lots of property to members in the community as well as donated land for relocation of Johnson Chapel A.M.E Church and for the black school in Malakoff, Texas. Zack leased his property (from the original 53.88 acres of land from his father) to the oil and gas industry on May 26, 1909. The land was leased to E.C. Hoadley.

After his death, the property was poorly maintained and was not followed up. The family lost the property. Zack was very generous and had lots of people living in the community purchasing lots or renting homes on his property. Those that he sold land to were; B. Barnes on February 16, 1934; Dan Gentry bought property in August 6, 1935, Hubbard Johnson October 7, 1935.

Zack traveled to Oklahoma in the early 1900's and married Sallie Menefee, in Stringtown, (Atoka County) Oklahoma. They were married on March 19, 1904.

This time frame could also account for the death of *Willie, since he was also "supposedly" living and working in Oklahoma for the railroad. He later worked in other cities like Tyler, Texas where he married his second wife, Lula Mayfield in 1920; no children were born to this Union. He met Vee Templeton while she was walking to church, and they married in August 4, 1928.

According to Faresa McCalister-Dawson, "My father was a Christian" and belonged to the local C.M.E. Church in Malakoff, Texas. He was a good man that loved all of his children. He would tell us fairy tales and ghost stories that kept them scared. He was a very comical man who loved playing practical jokes with them as children." He was a hard worker who took care of his farming and rental property in the community. Aunt Faresa says, "Yes I was spoiled by my dad, he would buy me shoes or anything I asked for, even though I did not need them when we went to town." She stated that this would get her in trouble with her mother when she returned home.

Aunt Zeola remembers that her father worked on the Barlett Ranch. His mode of transportation was a horse and he taught horseback riding to his children. He and his brothers were very close and they loved their family. They constantly visited each other. "Uncle Dixie" (Richard) and Daddy, would talk about their experiences growing up. Uncle Dixie lived two houses down from Zack.
Their parents, Isaah and Martha didn't believe in Banks therefore, they would bury their money in cans and hide it in the yard." "Our grandmother Martha was known as "Mrs. Malakoff". We were told by older citizens of

Malakoff that she was a society lady. She supported lots of projects financially.

"Daddy was a good provider. Daddy use to plant crops on our land. He planted Cotton, watermelon, peas, corn, and other vegetables. We never had to go to bed hungry. He would purchase fruit and vegetables in large quantities (ex) crates of apples, oranges, bushels of vegetables. After he stopped raising watermelons, he would buy a pickup load of watermelons. We always had appropriate clothing."

According to Aunt Zeola, "Daddy use to own a restaurant that he operated on weekends. He sold Bar-B-Que beef, pork and goat. The building was built on our land which was two blocks from the house (was next door to the location of Aunt Faresa's home).

Aunt Zeola also stated that "Daddy helped us with our homework. He was exceptionally good in math and could solve problems without using pencil and paper. He promoted self-esteem." Daddy and Mother had made plans to add on to our home place, lumber was purchased and suppose to be delivered the day our house burned completely destroying everything. Daddy phoned the lumber company and asked them to wait before delivering since he was going to rebuild the home. Instead, Daddy had another house built for our family. Later during the year daddy had a stroke, and never recovered.
According to Aunt Zeola, with the assistance of Uncle Dixie, daddy and he dug a well behind our house. Daddy bricked the walls of the well and cemented the bottom leaving only a hole at the bottom of the well for the spring to come through. The well was approximately 15-20 feet deep. The well supplied all of our water needs. Some residents from Malakoff would come and draw water from

our well. They would say the water had a good taste and was cool and refreshing.

According to Zack's daughters and his death certificate, Zack stayed in a coma from May 23, 1945 to May 26, 1945 (4 days). Aunt Zeola remembers him waking up briefly and looking toward someone and replied he would be ready to leave at 3:00pm. Zack then closed his eyes and died that afternoon at 2:00 pm.

Well-Known Negro Paralysis Victim

Zack McCalister, well-known Malakoff negro suffered a paralytic stroke during the night Monday which left him unconscious and in a very critical condition. He was found in a shed near his home about 7:00 o'clock Tuesday morning by other negros who had spent the greater part of the night searching for him.

The negro, who had been working as janitor for a number of business houses up town, failed to show up at his home at the usual time following his day's work Monday, and when his absence at a late hour was still unaccounted for, neighbors set out looking for him. The shed in which he was found, was some distance beyond his home on Highway 31, and it is not known just how he came to wonder off there, instead of going home, which had been his usual custom. It was believed that he had gone to the shed earlier in the afternoon and that he had remained there in the cold, damp air throughout the night.

Willie, who was six at the time, remembers going to feed the livestock's with his father and helping his dad gather up the apple and oranges from their fruit trees.

Zack married Vee Templeton in Malakoff Texas in August 4, 1928. To this Union they had seven children and *one daughter from a previous relationship. The children are:

1. *Ella Mae McCalister Payne (mom unknown)
2. Faresa McCalister Dawson
3. Maurice McCalister
4. Zeola McCalister Johnson
5. E.H. McCalister
6. Shirley McCalister
7. Rev. Willie McCalister
8. Dr. Joe McCalister

Shirley

Maurice McCalister

Young Negro Is County's 7th. Traffic Victim

A ten-year-old negro boy Saturday was Henderson County's first traffic fatality in several months and the seventh death during 1941 for this county.
The boy, Maurice McCallister, son of Jack McCallister, of near Malakoff, was riding in a wagon on Highway 31 with a crowd of colored people Saturday afternoon about four o'clock, Constable D. B. Billings, of Malakoff, reported. The child was in the rear of the wagon, Mr. Billings said, and as an automobile approached meeting the wagon, he jumped off the rear and ran across the highway into the path of the motor vehicle. A. A. Hicks, of Jasper, Texas, driver of the automobile saw the boy to late to avoid hitting him.
The child succumbed seven hours later, at 11 o'clock, according to Billings. No arrest was made in connection with the accident, the driver of the automobile being absolved of blame, Billings reported.

E.H., Zeola, Willie, Faresa, Vee (Wife) and Joe McCalister

Dr. Joe, Ella May, Vee, E.H., Zeola, Faresa, Rev. Willie McCalister

Vee Templeton McCalister
September 1, 1907- May 15, 2011

102 years ago, on September 1, 1907, Vee McCalister was born in Kilgore, Texas to the parents of Tom and Bessie Templeton. She was the oldest of 14 children (seven boys and seven girls). The only surviving sibling is her youngest sister, Dorothy Templeton. Vee was a very obedient child, attended church regularly and also took on several leadership roles in the church including Secretary, Missionary President and Treasurer of the Sunday school. Vee and Zack met and were married on August 4, 1928. They had seven children, named: Faresa, Maurice McCalister, Zeola, E.H., Shirley, Willie, and Joe McCalister. Zack had a daughter named Ella Mae whom Vee raised.

Vee has always placed a value on her family, and they mean more than anything else in life. Zack had an untimely death, and Vee realized that life would not be easy without her husband, but born with a strong will and faith, she knew she would be able to provide for her children. She was the first African American in her town to purchase a television, and later placed it in the window bringing dozens of guests nightly to watch TV from her yard as if they were in a movie theater.

Vee attended one year of college at Central Texas College in Waco which was affiliated with the Baptist church. This College was created for African Americans which is now defunct. The college was not accredited degree granting institution, but it was a school were black students were to complete a formal high school course of instructions. According to Jessie May Payne Bullock (Vee McCalister roommate), during that time in rural Texas communities, local public schools for African Americans did not usually take students through 12 complete grades of academic instruction. Therefore many students were sent here to complete their education. In 1992, Jessie said that Central Texas College and Guadeloupe College were equivalent of the 1990's junior colleges.

Central State College was founded in Waco, Texas in 1902 by the Central Texas Academy by black Baptists church. This College closed in 1931 due to financial difficulties. There are no landmarks for this school due to a U.S. Highway 81 was built over the grounds in 1951 where the college campus site was located.
Vee McCalister Toles (later remarried Rev. Tole) gave notice in the Athens Daily Review, a newspaper of general circulation for Henderson County, Texas dated April 12, 1954 filed an application for authority to make, execute and deliver an oil, gas and mineral lease with pooling or unitization provision on the land. The lessee was C. W. Cory.

She encouraged her children to get an education and to make something of their lives. She planted and cultivated a huge field of vegetable and fruits which she used to feed her family. She also created her own business by making Ms. Vee's special hair ointment, guaranteed to tame your hair, make your hair grow and become thick. Individuals and families throughout the city and in other towns purchased Ms. Vee's hair ointment for years. She even paid a small commission to two of her grandchildren to serve as salespersons delivering the handmade hair ointment to customers.

At the age of 102, Vee McCalister enjoys reading and having discussions on politics, the economy and Black History. She also voted in the historical 2008 Presidential election of President Obama. She thanks God for allowing her to build a new home and to pay for it herself. She often speaks of how so many people want to use illness, poor finances and being a single mom as a crutch. She often shares with friends and family that she has experienced it all, but if you believe and trust in God and always keep your faith strong …. God will deliver you through any situation.

Vee McCalister was the oldest and last member of the second generation, who married into the McCalister family.

Rev. Willie McCalister

My Dad, Rev. Willie McCalister was asked to submit a family DNA test to determine our family ethnicity matches. The results of the test were as follows:

Regions: Nigeria 41%, Ivory Coast/Ghana 18%, Mali 15%, Cameroon/Congo 5%, Benin/Togo 4%, America 2%, Africa South-Central Hunter-Gatherers 2%, Africa Southeastern Bantu 2%, Europe at 11%, Iberian Peninsula 5%, Scandinavia 3%, Ireland 1%, Great Britain 1%, Italy/Greece 1%, and Native American 2%.

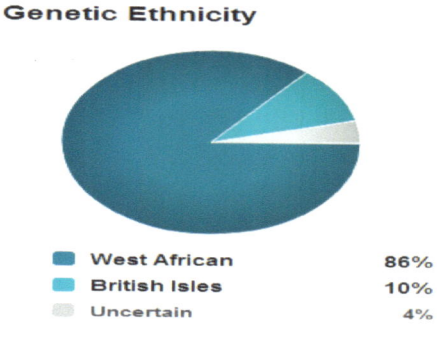

Rev. Willie McCalister begin preaching in The Central Texas Conference in 1959, admitted to trail in the November 1961 conference. He was a delegate for the 1970 General Conference from Central Texas Conference. He was an alternate delegate for the 1974 General Conference from Dallas and Fort Worth Texas Conference. Dallas Fort Worth, Texas annual Conference July 7-11, 1975 Rev. Willie McCalister is the Conference Secretary. He was a delegate for the 1977 General Conference from Dallas Fort Worth, Texas annual Conference, Delegate for Dallas Fort Worth annual Conferences and Central Texas Conference.

Powell Chapel no longer exist Kerns Texas (He followed Dr. Rev. Jimmy Clark); Thompson Chapel no longer exist, Jacksonville, Texas; Mt. Zion, Carthage, Texas; Vivian Chapel, Longview, Texas; Beckville Texas Bethel CME church; Union Chapel Gladwater, Texas (Married my Mom when he became the minister here); Promise Land, Canton, Texas; Miles Chapel Crockett, Texas; Wesley Chapel, Henderson Texas 1966-1967 Central TX conference; Christian Chapel Dallas, Texas; Carter Metropolitan July 12-16, 1976, Fort Worth, Texas; Cedar Crest Dallas, Texas; and Miles Chapel Tyler, Texas.

Bishops he served under were:

Bishop Henry Phillips Porter 1950-1958, Bishop Bertram W. Doyle 1958-1966, Bishop Norris S. Curry 1966-1967, Bishop Caesar David Coleman 1974, Bishop Cunningham, Bishop Gilmore, and Bishop Williamson.

Presiding Elders:

T.O. Green, **N.B. Stewart**, **Jesse J. Thompson**, **Frank Wesley Bendy** (transferred to the East Tex Conference under him) **Danner**, **Moore** (transferred to Central Tex

Conference), **Rev. Percy Luther Gray** 1966 conference, **J.O. Morton, J.C.Darden, C.N. Reed, Donald Matlock, C.W. Morehead** (gave him an appointment in his conference)

Promised Land was one of the best churches he has ever had growing up in the ministry. He only stayed at this church a year.

Other *McCalister's in this Conference November 1944 Alonzo McCallister was admitted on trial.

Waters Chapel, originated in the Oak Hill Community in 1932, 12 miles northeast of Henderson, Texas. The first services were held in the Oak Hill School and the first revival was held on the present church ground under a brush arbor with Mrs. Tuggle as evangelist.

The Pastor was J.W. Waters. Faithful members who helped the church grow were George White, his wife and Enoch McAllister, the chairperson of the Steward Board and Rev. Alonzo McAllister. Church location is on highway farm road 782 a mile from its original location.

*I only have information for some of the churches that family members attended.

Willie/William McCalister
September 1887 – unknown

Willie McCalister was born in September 1887 in Malakoff, Texas. Willie was the fourth child born to Martha and Isaah McCalister. Not much information is known about Willie.

I asked Aunt Faresa about him, and she stated that her father said he was an engineer of some sorts; he was a very inventive man, smart and loved to create things. According to her father, he worked with the railroad and created parts for the train. He was killed around the 1900's in Oklahoma by a train which notified the family of his death. Zack and his mother when to Oklahoma to retrieve the body, but found out they had already buried it.

There is no other information on Willie. According to the census records in 1910, Martha is listed as a widow with ten children living and 2 decease.

* I am currently still checking patent records, Railroad, and other sources to find out information about his life.
Mrs. Donnie Barron Berry, (married a minister Rev. O.D. Barron) who was a member at Carter Metropolitan, stated that he could crack a hickory nut with his mouth. The only man she knew who could do that.

Cleveland Sherman McCalister
August 13, 1890 – June 24, 1962

Cleveland McCalister was the fifth son born to Isaah and Martha McCalister. Cleveland became a major leader with the McCalister brothers.

He seems to have been in charge of keeping the family land ownership in the family after the death of his parents. Most of the property was left for him to inform family members to pay taxes and for the rental property individuals to pay their monthly rent. He was responsible for all the family land ownership.

According to the Malakoff's City Council, an offer to purchase a small lot at the end of Moss Street for extension in the amount of $3,500.00 for a right-of-way for a street leading to the new sewer plant site. This lot amount of 81 x 100 feet near the Cotton Belt Railroad. Mayor A. M. Thompson informed the City Council that this was private property, and recommended the purchase. In return it would be fenced and accessed to the proposed plant across the tracks will be through a locked gate.

Cleveland was married to Rosie Henry.

Cleveland worked for the Railroad …. The children of Cleveland and Rosie were:
1. Trula McCalister Black
2. James McCalister "Son" married Sarah Payne who is also from Malakoff, Texas. In the Payne genealogy history, she and her family (James Jr, and Floyda) lived with Isaah and Martha Payne's family when first married on their family farm.

3. Cleo McCalister Walton

4. Marvin McCalister
5. Eddie McCalister
6. Helen McCalister
7. Cleveland McCalister Jr. "June" was the baby boy of the family. He attended college in Tyler, Texas at the age of 16 but was unable to complete school. He married Mary Ann White in 1950 and they later moved to Dayton, Ohio. There were blessed with four children. Cleveland retired from General Motors in 1982 after 30 years of services. He was a businessman who owned a drapery shop. He loved his western gear and would often be seen with his cowboy's hat, boots and western belt buckle. He and his family were members of the Greater Allen A.M.E church.

Cleveland McCalister granted a right of way for a street leading to the new sewer plant to Malakoff's City Council in a special meeting when a proposal was made to buy a lot on Moss Street for $3,500. This transaction occurred in 1977.

Moddie D. McCalister
June 24, 1895-
December 18, 1948

Moddie D. McCalister, the sixth son of Isaah and Martha's McCalister, was born on June 24, 1895 and died on December 18, 1948.

Moddie had a heart attack after preaching his sermon in Mt. Comfort C.M.E Church, in Overton, Texas. Rev. Moddie McCalister was a minister of passion. He served the state of Texas as a delegate for General Conferences and is shown on pictures with the ministers who were involved in the C.M.E. church conference from the 1940's.

Rev. Moddie preached and proclaimed the word of God. He also served as a community staunch support for the Black families in the community. According to the Payne's family history in 1921 or 1922, two carloads of Ku Klux Klan's members were dressed in white robes and their faces were covered by hoods visited Hayes Place on the Tidmore farm near Malakoff, Texas. They said they were looking for a man name Marty (Moddie) McCalister and asked Hayes Paynes where Marty lived. Hayes responded that he didn't know, and the Klansmen drove away without incident. According to Hayes, Moddie lived on a farm only a few miles beyond Hayes's House. It was not known if the Klan ever made contact with Moddie.

Moddie and his brother Charlie are later shown with land deeds leasing property near the same oil fields where his mom Martha had made her fortune. Both (Moddie and Charlie) men sold their land.

Like his brothers. M.D. McCalister became a landowner who purchased property from W. E. Phillip on lot number 14 in the W.E. Phillips third addition to the town of Malakoff, Texas. He purchased this property on April 19, 1927.

He moved to Jacksonville, Texas while doing his ministry at the C.M.E. Church.

Rev. Moddie McCalister was the Presiding Elder of the Tyler District with Appointments from 1938-1939.

Churches that were under his directives were: St. James Station (Tyler) Mt. Zion and Chandler, Larissia and South Tyler, Church Hill, Mt. Haven, Crockett and Halls Bluff, Palestine Circuit, Bullard and Cuney Mission, Malakoff Circuit which include Brookings (Brookins) Chapel, and Corinth (K.C. Phillips minister) Kerens circuit, Pennell Chapel and Holly Springs, Corinth Circuit which include Corinth, Grapeland, Neches., Mt. Zion and Trinity Circuit As of November 26-30 1941 Texas Conference M.D. McCallister (sp incorrect) is still in the Tyler District.

November 12, 1944 Ministers assignment W.D. McAlister (sp incorrect M.D.) pastor of Miles Chapel, Tyler Texas. As of 1966 -1967 Tyler district had Mt. Haven and Larissa churches still in existence. They also had Malakoff and Corinth (Malakoff Circuit, and Kerns and Brookins (Kerns Circuit).

Moddie married Savannah Johnson on February 4, 1912 in Henderson County, Texas. To this union, they were blessed with children who are listed below. The children names are:

1. Essie McCalister

2. Spatsie D. McCalister was the first Black man elected Marshal of Caney City and Deputy Marshal. He was also the owner of Mack's Landing.

3. Lee Ander McCalister was born on December 10, 1917 in Malakoff, Texas. He was the second son of Savannah and Moddie McCalister. He was a graduate of Texas College and Prairie view A&M College where he earned his Masters. He taught school at Lindale from 1941-1947. Lee Ander was also a principal of Blackshear and Central Elementary school in Lamesa, Texas in August 1955 per the Big Spring Herald newspaper. He continued his studies at St. Louise University, Texas Tech University, University of New Mexico and Sul Ross University, Alpine, Texas. On March 1960, he became an area captain for Cancer Crusade in Dawson County.

> **L.A. MCCALISTER**
> Funeral services for Lee Ander McCalister, 65, of Lamesa are scheduled for 2:30 p.m. Tuesday at the New Hope CME Church in Malakoff with the Rev. D.R. Madlock and the Rev. Tomy Starks officiating.
> Burial will follow in the Steen Cemetery under the direction of Brown's Mortuary of Malakoff.
> Mr. McCalister died at his home after a short illness.
> He was born Dec. 10, 1917 in Malakoff. He was a graduate of Texas College and Prairieview A&M College. He taught school at Lindale and was principal of Blackshear and Central Elementary Schools in Lamesa. At the time of his death he was director of Special Services for Lamesa Public Schools.
> Survivors include his wife, Lillian McCalister; one daughter, Moddie McCalister, Jr.; two brothers, Spatsie McCalister and Rev. Denoyd McCalister; his step-mother, Mrs. L.B. McCalister and two grandchildren.

4. Elbert McCalister was born on October 17, 1919 in Malakoff, Texas
5. Rev. Venoyd McCalister followed his dad in the ministry. He became the Presiding Elder of the 8th Episcopal District, Resident presiding Elder, Longview-Marshall conference, member of the Texas College Trustee Board, Member of the General Board of Personnel Services, and Member of the committee of Episcopacy.

Elder Venoyd McCalister

Elder Venoyd McCalister preached at some of the following churches: Beckville Texas, Post Oak CME church was also built by Venoyd McCalister. Post Oak

Longview, TX 1966-1967 (Presiding Elder N.B. Stewart); Venoyd built Hynson Chapel in Winnsboro, TX, Webster CME Church, Winnsboro, TX, He built Wesley Chapel Greenville, TX, Lone Oak CME.

The East Texas Annual Conference meeting chose Venoyd McCalister as a Clerical Delegate for the General Conference held in 1962. He was a delegate for the 1970 General Conference from East Texas Conference. He was an alternate delegate for the 1974 General Conference from Central Texas Conference. He was a delegate for the 1977 General Conference from East Texas Conference.

After the death of his wife, Moddie married Lela Bell Scott who was born October 1, 1907 in Tyler, Texas.

Venoyd McCalister- Father and Son

Our dad was Venoyd McCalister. His father was Moddie D. McCalister. Venoyd married Maenette Garner and Moddie married Savannah Johnson.

Venoyd and Maenette raised six children in their union. They are:

a) Cora Jean, Venoyd Jr., Mac Neil, Gloria Annette, Lanier Winston,
b) Deborah Ann McCalister

Moddie and Savannah Johnson raised three boys, losing a baby daughter who passed away in her infancy. Boys were Spatsy, Leander, and Venoyd McCalister (all deceased). Venoyd was five years old when his mother Savannah died, leaving very young children to Moddie's care.

Venoyd's father, the Reverend Moddie D. McCalister remarried Ms. Lela Bell Scott. Venoyd followed in his father's footsteps and became an ordained Methodist Minister serving the Lord for many years.

As a young boy, Venoyd missed his father and stepmother as service in the church meant frequent travel. As Venoyd grew into a young man, he soon became a star football player at Malakoff High School, Malakoff, Texas.

Moddie had a home built in Jacksonville, Texas for his new wife and sons. When Venoyd married Maenette, they lived on the same property in a small home owned by his father. Cora and Venoyd still remember living next door to Grand Daddy Moddie.
Venoyd served in the U.S. Army during World War II and was stationed in France. Grand Daddy Moddie watched over Venoyd's family while he was away during the war.

Grand Daddy Moddie died in December 1948 of a heart attack.

As living heirs of these great men, we are indeed blessed. We will forever hold them dear.
Love,
Gloria A McCalister-Pringle
September 10, 2003

Charlie Kirksey McCalister
July 30, 1892- December 14, 1943

Charlie McCalister was the seventh son born to Isaah and Martha McCalister. He was born on July 30, 1892.

Charlie was married to Emma Graves McCalister in Malakoff, Texas. Emma Graves McCalister was born 1892 and died 1946. To this blessed union, the children that were born to them are:
1. Jenell McCalister
2. Alcie McCalister at age 2 years of age contracted Poliomyelitis and unable to walk.
3. Martha McCalister
4. Charlie T
5. Charlie Kirk

Charlie McCalister was born in July of 1892 (he never knew the exact date and celebrated his birthday on July 31) and he was the seventh child of Isaah and Martha McCalister. On October 19, 1913, he was married to Emma Graves. He attended public school in Malakoff, Texas and had to stop after finishing the third grade to work in the fields. Because he was unable to finish school, he was very strict about his children doing their homework and getting an education. As an adult, he was a farmer in Oakwood, Texas and worked in the brickyards in Malakoff, Texas. He attended C.M.E. Methodist Church.
Charlie died December 14, 1943.

Remembering my father

My father, Charlie McCalister, was a very kind, honest and hardworking man who did his best to provide for his family. I remember the very happy Saturday nights with homemade ice cream. On Sunday evenings, Charlie enjoyed playing baseball with his children and the neighborhood children. At night we often played checkers and he "cheated" if he was "losing". Playing marbles with his son was one of his favorite.

Charlie had a very strong beliefs and convictions. He enjoyed arguing religious issues with members of other denominations. He often referred to his oldest son in law, LaFred Gibson, as a "hard shelled Baptist", but we all knew that he (Charlie) was a "hard shelled Methodist". He sincerely believed that baptism by immersion was not essential to salvation. As a result, his children were sprinkled at a very young age. They were later baptized by immersion because my mother Emma was reared in the Baptist faith and did not share his beliefs. He sincerely believed that women and girls should be respected, protected and never hit by men.

Because of this belief, when we disobeyed, he would say "I'm going to tell your mama". Our discipline was always done by our mother.
He enjoyed planting crops of cotton, corn, peanuts, peas, etc... and watching them grow. He spent long hours taking care of the farm animals. He often went hunting and fishing for fun and food. Charlie was a very happy person and would sing, even if he was having a bad day.

We loved him very much.
Bio written by: Charlie Theresa McCalister Campbell July 1994.

Charlie T. McCalister

Charlie Theresa McCalister was born on October 3, 1921 in Oakwood, Texas. She was the fourth child of Charlie and Emma McCalister. She attended Lockland Elementary School in Malakoff, Texas. Her parents moved back to Oakwood, Texas, therefore her high school years were spent at St. Paul High School. It was a new High School with a gymnasium built in the St. Paul area. She graduated number one in her class in 1938. Early McCalister built a large white house near the high school and she stayed with them to attend high school. She and her cousin Catherine walked to school together each day. That was the best school that they had ever gone to, going to different rooms and teachers for each class.

In 1943, she became the bride of Cleveland Campbell. From this union eight children were born. They were married for twenty-seven years until his death on August 19, 1969.

Charlie T. is a Methodist at heart and raised her children in that faith, taking them to Sunday school and Church every Sunday. She instilled in them a belief in Christ, good moral values and good work ethics. She believed strongly in education and as a result made sure that all of her children attended college.

She enjoys spending quiet evenings at home reading, doing crossword puzzles, watching TV games shows and playing dominoes with her children. Although she has slowed down, she still likes to travel and attends many of the Senior Citizen events held in the city, still driving her own car.

This was written in a journal to her grandchildren.

Richard "Uncle Dixie "Dean McCalister
January 31, 1894-July 13, 1956

Richard McCalister was the eight son born to Isaah and Martha McCalister. Uncle Dixie, nickname affectionately for Richard was a very intelligent man. Richard was married to Jewel E. Harris-McCalister-Morgan and they had no children.

Aunt Zeola remembers her dad Zack telling them about Richard's as an inventor of sorts and how he invented the part for the railroad brakes used on trains. He went to Oklahoma to patent his invention and somehow when he applied it was stolen from him (currently researching that information) and he did not receive his credit. Aunt Zeola, whom I interviewed about Richard, said he was a mechanical man. He was a Carpenter, Mechanical Engineer and Architect.

"Uncle Dixie was really a nice man and often came to their home talking about his work and scaring her and her siblings. She stated that when he visited their father, they would tell ghost stories and joke with each other all night long and Uncle E.H. and Willie McCalister would have to take him home. They would run back home after getting him home. They were a close family.

I also interviewed my dad, Rev. Willie McCalister. My dad stated he was Richard's collection driver, this was his first job that he loved to do since they went to home collecting payment for rent, or auto repairs. Dad stated that Richard was also a Mechanic, and was one of the first black persons in Malakoff, Texas to own a vehicle it was a Duce burgh.

Daddy said all of the brothers were some of the best entrepreneurs and knew how to handle their business.

Richard and his wife had no children. He made the railroad car that two men were riding on. He invented this however he did not received the credit. Malakoff was known as the lignite city and the coal was used with this contraption that he created.

Richard Dixie McCalister was a Private First Company, First Battalion 165th Depot Brigade in the Army of the United States. Richard enlisted in the army at the age of 24 7/12 years of age occupation was an Auto Mechanic at Camp Travis, Texas on November 15, 1918. He was discharged as of February 2, 1951.

* I am currently still checking patent records, Railroad, and other sources to find out information about his life. According to family members, Richard worked for Kirby Automotive repairing cars and he was very good at those repairs. When he died, his widow Jewel McCalister moved in the home of Vee McCalister until she was able to buy another home to live in. It seems that the brothers wanted to make sure that the property stayed in the family and uprooted her from the home she had created with Richard her spouse.

Larrissie McCalister
February 20, 1896- February 20, 1954

Larrissie was the ninth son and the baby of the family and he had a bit of a temper than all of the other children. He had several scrapes with the law but was successful in providing for his family.

Larrissie was married to Lillian Murray and were blessed with children who are named:
1. I.H. (Hillory) McCalister
2. Eugene McCalister
3. Willie McCalister

Larrissie was also a landowner per his father's probate records. He begins selling his land to the community of Malakoff, Texas. He sold land to W. B. James on December 5, 1936. According to the Census, Larrissie was still living with his mother until she died in 1925.

I enjoyed talking to family members and one of his best friends about Larrissie exploits, and his brother's attempts to calm him down. Larrissie was a man who did not take any stuff from anyone. He did not like to be threatened or did not want to see his family struggling.

I interviewed his best friend, Hurley Anderson in 2000 with Vickie Johnson and Nicole Johnson present. According to Hurley, Larrissie had a bit of a temper when he was angered. He was threaten in a barber shop by Arthur who claimed he was going to shoot him, so when he was getting his hair cut, the guy made a move and Hurley said Larrissie shot him. This made news in Malakoff, Texas. Larrissie was sentenced to two years in Huntsville, Texas on March 5, 1932. On March 18, 1933 Governor Ferguson granted him a full Pardon.

Larrissie served in the military and perhaps this could have been an additional source of much of his anger.
He stayed in trouble with the law when he consumed alcohol. It made him meaner. According to my dad, he remembers his daddy having to tie his brother to the tree to keep him from fighting. He would remain tied to the tree until he sobered up and lost the desire to fight. Aunt Zeola remembers her daddy telling her that he had a hard, head and he would get so mad that he once butted a plank off a house.

Like all of his brothers, he loved his family and constantly visited his family to discuss farming, land transactions, and other family concerns.

According to family oral tradition, Larrissie was not religious however; he died with the bible on his chest leading family members to believe he was studying and perhaps maintained a relationship with God. His daughter Willie had the bible and when she died the bible was given to members of Charlie T's Campbell family who still have it today. Arlene Ricks now has the bible others are scared to have it since it rumored that whoever has it in their possession has died very young. I am requesting pictures and perhaps the bible to keep in the family.

The Malakoff News

clares that the Col. has made good on all of his campaign promises, made when running for mayor, and that he will do for Texas what he has done for the city of Amarillo.

Two Negros Arrested Charged With Hog Theft

Larrissa McCalister and Rich Jackson, (col) were lodged in jail here Wednesday morning on a charge of stealing hogs, said to have been the property of J. W. Robertson.

A white man, while coon hunting Tuesday night, saw the two negros killing a number of hogs and returned to town and reported the incident to local officers. Constable A. W. Leopard, at three o'clock Wednesday morning, drove to the home of Rich Jackson where he found one of the animals hanging, already cleaned. McCalister had already left the Jackson place, and the officer followed his wagon tracks which led him to McCalister home in the negro quarters, west of town. There, in a side room of the house were six freshly killed, uncleaned hogs.

The animals were restored to their owner Wednesday morning, who prepared them for storage.

Nacogdoches Negro Fatally Injured In Christmas Eve Row

Larrissie McCalister Charged With Shooting, Makes Bond For $1,000.

Arthur Ballenger, negro laborer belonging to one of the rail road construction crews stationed at Wofford, was fatally wounded by a bullet from a 38 automatic in the hands of Larrissie McCalister in the Govan barber shop in west Malakoff Christmas Eve night. The bullet took effect in the right side of the neck ranging downward and lodged in the spine. He was immediately brought to the city for medical attention and was then carried to the camp. He died Wednesday night while he was being taken, by his uncle, to his home at Nacogdoches.

McCalister was taken into custody by local officers following the shooting and brought before R. A. McLain, Justice of the Peace where he waived examining trial. He was released on of $1,000.00 to await the next session of the District Court.

CHAPTER 11 Meet The Henry's

Thomas and Oma Henry were the parents of:
1. Martha Henry
2. Hiram (Mary Hubbard 2nd Irene)
3. Grant (Lozie Wiley)
4. Thomas
5. Mary
6. Lamay (Lanny) (Elris Whatley)
7.

Martha

Martha's parents Thomas and Oma Henry ingrained in their daughter and other children their skills since they were also lucrative landowners. The families were staunch supporters of New Hope CME church and donated land for the Antioch Cemetery in Malakoff, Texas. This cemetery is one of the oldest Black cemeteries on the western end of the Henderson County.

The original property is located on what was known as Yarabee Ranch which is now known as Yarabee Ranch Road which is off of highway 90, south of Malakoff, Texas. This land belonged to John Thomas Henry and his wife Oma Henry. John sold this land to the trustees of Methodist Church whose primary goals were to build a church, New Hope C.M.E. for the growing community. The Trustees, John Windfield, Wesley Brookins, and Pres Brown paid the sum of $10.00 for 2 acres. The prior deed owner was J.W. Smooth who owned 150 acres track of land situated on the waters of Walnut Creek known as Ligon League. This transaction was on February 27, 1883. This Land sale established New Hope Christian Methodist Church and it created a burial ground for the African American Community.

The community was known as Antioch which became the name for the new Cemetery. A log cabin Church was built and named New Hope CME. This church serviced the community for several years until many of the members moved farther away. Because of its location, many of the members eventually moved closer into Malakoff, Texas and built several new churches.

New Hope CME bought another plot of land from Ben Urey where they begin building a new Log Cabin church. The original location was now set aside as a cemetery and many of the community people were now buried on the present day location.

A historical monument is now located in the Antioch Cemetery today as a testimony of her family contribution to the African American community.

Martha's first marriage was to a William Pinkard on October 10, 1874 in Limestone County in 1870 where Thomas and his family lived prior to moving to Henderson County, Texas.
Martha was already with child, Oma McCalister when she married Issah McCalister. This information was based on her marriage license, administered by Sandy McCalister and the birth of Oma McCalister.

When Isaah died in 1907, Martha married Leo Fletcher and divorced him and years later married Solomon Larson on January 27, 1920 by Jeff C. Davis.

According to the census Martha actually gave birth to thirteen children wth only sevem living as of 1910 Census.

May 26, 1909 Martha leased the land to E.C. Hoadley for gas, oil lines. This land was very prosperous and rich with oil. The property was lost due to failure to pay taxes, and basically stolen from the family.

In the later years, Zack McCalister family attempted to take the company to court but lost their case due to failure to maintain proper landowner agreements.

Martha McCalister became a lucrative realtor and begin selling property to locals. She begin selling plots to individuls like Elvira Green in the amount of $100.00 todays worth $1,412.4. This deed record was on January 19, 1919.

Due to oil and gas leases, Martha forgot to pay the taxes on her property and on August 1, 1926 a Certificate of Redemption for a demand letter to pay delinquent State and County Taxes on her property. She had to pay $32.11 to S. H. Terrell Comptroller office in Austin, Texas for 77 acres on the Peter Tumlinson survey and 53 acres on the Ligon survey.

1880 Census has Thomas Henry at age 64, Oma at age 48, Hiram, Grant, Thomas, Mary

1900 Census Grant Henry is 28 married to Lozie Wiley children: Roxie, Merrick, Salena

1910 Census Hiram marries Mary Hubbard at 18, children: Feluasar daughter, Clemming Hubbard stepdaughter, Baley Hubbard stepson.

1910 Oklahoma census Pittsburg County, Grant H. Henry is 39 and widow living with: Elris Whatley children: Lamay Whatley.
Grant's children are:

Rocksy dau, Merrick son, Jiles (Jules) son, Myrtle daughter

1920- State of Oklahoma Lincoln County Cimarron census report.

Henry Grant is 46 and remarried to Irene 39 children: Merrick 21, Myrtle 20, Jules 18, Alvan B 18,Ollia B 24, Gusaic 19,Calvan J. 4,Elbert 2, Afatola 3 Capatola

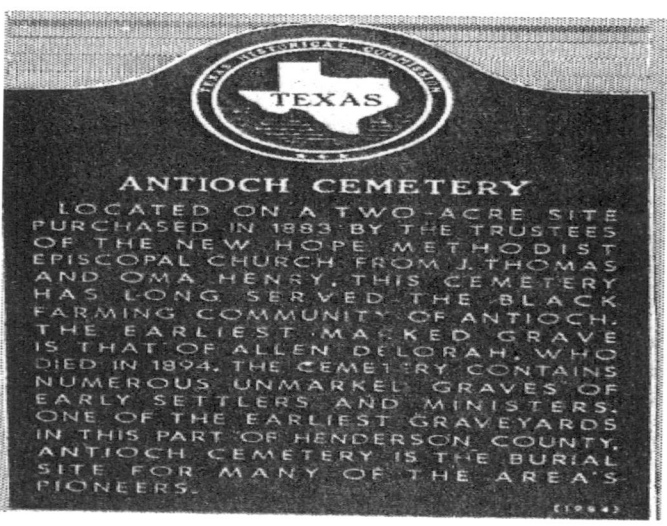

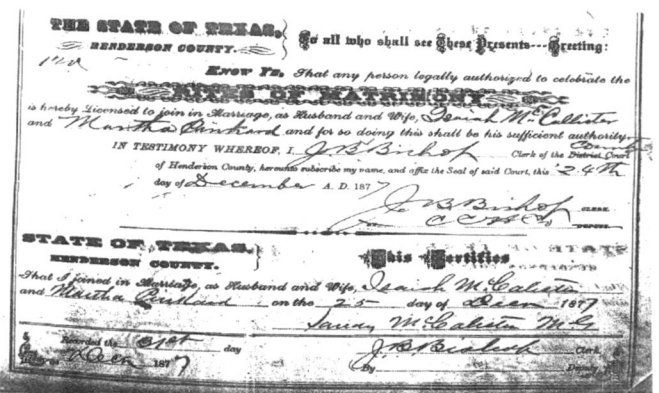

CHAPTER 12 Family Homestead

While talking to family members, I received information from my Father, Willie and Faresa McCalister regarding the home that the family lived in. These homes were popular in Texas plains and were called the "Dog Trot". This type of home had a central, open hallway that separated two distinct portions of the house. This dog-trot was accessible to all.

The home consisted of two single living quarters separated by a passageway that opens at both ends all beneath a common roof. It enclosed two sides of which has a living room by a wall, and shared bedrooms. The roof covered the entire house. The hallway was exposed to the elements at both ends. While wind, rain, dust, sleet and snow found their way into the hallway, the summer breezes provided natural air conditioning from the Texas heat.

My dad, Rev. Willie McCalister recalls that the house was very large and was able to accommodate everyone.

The house was built about one to three feet above the ground and had the kitchen on the far left side of the house.

Rev. Willie McCalister said that they lived on the right side of the house. This was the living quarters for the children and parents. Larrissie still lived in the house which was around 1933 according to the Malakoff, Texas newspaper which verifies a little information about the structure of the house during one of his infamous exploits.

 Cleveland McCalisters Home

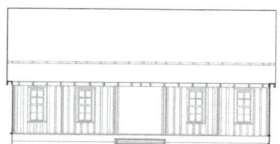

Larrissie was the last person to live in the home. As a child my dad remembers playing around the old dilapidated house and was astonished how large it appears to have been. The structure of the home was referred to as a Dog Trot.

Houses that are simliar to the one Isaah owned.

Chapter 13 Family Medical History

Family most common health ailments are:

Thrombosis and Pulmonary Embolism	Myocardial infarction	Diabetes
Sudden Cardiac Death	Angina	Diabetic comma
Endocarditic	Aortic Dissection	Cancer
Heart Disease (Coronary Artery Disease)	Heart Murmur	Cirrhosis of the liver
	Arrhythmia	Heart Attack
	High Blood Pressure	High Blood pressure
	Congestive Heart Failure	Cerebral Hemorrhages
	Myocarditis	Arteriovenous
	Stroke	Coronary Occlusion

CHAPTER 14 Henderson County, Texas Black Communities

Black Ministers from 1871-1882
Moses Chaffin
Mack Richardson
Sandy McCalister
Richard McCalister
Benjamin F. Miller

Black Communities
Caney city was once known as Larkin Farm bought by Dr. Larkin's for his freed slaves to live on. The quarters were known as Lick Skillet. Share croppers were between Dr. W.C. Larkin and Nat Coleman after 1865.
Log Cabin addition
Flatwood
Crosswood
Willow Spring may have begun in the early 1850's and owned by Nat P. Coleman. This location was where we first find Mariana and her family living. It is located 7 ½ miles southwest of Athens and bordered by Beck's Chapel, Cross Roads, Post Oak and Rome.
Antioch
Moore Station
Saint Paul
Turkey creek
Stockard

Black Churches:

New Hope Corinth C.M.E. Church History
An organizational meeting for the New Hope Christian Methodist Episcopal Church was held in 1910. The New Hope was founded and built by Rev. A.M. Hall, 1917. The charter members were Press B. Brown, W.F. Blair, Oliver T. Thomas and Dewitt B. Brookins who served as trustee and Stewards. Rev. E.E. Dunn was responsible for the right of ways for the church to be moved. With the aid a few members, and the donation of lumber, the first church as erected on what is known as St. Paul Drive, Four blocks North of West Royal Blvd. That church was moved to its present site in 1940 under the pastorate of Rev. K.C. Phillips. Rev. J.C. Henry, Rev. Morland and Rev. George Land were later pastors.

In 1961, a tornado came through Malakoff and destroyed several structures. New Hope was one of those buildings. It did not completely destroy the building but it eventually became unsafe to worship in. In 1963, Rev. George Jones was assigned to New Hope. Under his leadership, the congregation held worship services in Johnson Chapel A.M.E. Church. This worked out well because Johnson Chapel had alternating services as well. New Hope Pastoral days were first and third Sundays and Johnson Chapel pastoral days were second and fourth.

Out of tragedy, a bond was formed between the members of both churches that still remain. While waiting for the church to be rebuilt, the pastor and members tore down the damaged church, pulled nails, and raised funds. Rev. Jones remained until the Annual conference in 1965 where they assigned Rev. J.E. Mathis to New Hope.
 On July 15, 1965, a building committee was called together to discuss the status of the church. Members of

this committee were: Curtis Barron, Ira Green, A.J. Baron, and Nathan Barron. Rev. Mathis took ill in the middle of the conferences year and Rev. Gain was briefly assigned to New Hope. In 1966, Rev. George Griffin became the pastor. On September 12, 1967, a special meeting was called by Presiding Elder, Percy L. Gray to make plans to rebuild New Hope. Members of this committee were: R. D. Barron Sr., Ira Green, R. D. Barron Jr., A. J. Barron, Curtis Barron, and Nathan Barron. This committee worked diligently under the leadership of Bishop Norris Curry and Rev. George Griffin, Dedicatory Service was held May 21, 1968.

There was three other C.M.E. Churches in the area. New Hope was considered the station Church therefore when the membership and building were destroyed Brookins and Corinth were asked to merge with New Hope. Brookins and Corinth met once a month and all three churches shared the same pastor. Since Corinth merged in 1995, New Hope added the name Corinth to their name. New Hope became New Hope Corinth C.M.E. Church. This merger was a smooth transition for both congregations.

Corinth C.M.E Church, (Rome CME Church) Rev. Hodge, located at Cross Roads. Crossroad is located off Highway 198 about 10 miles from Malakoff, Texas. Corinth merged with New Hope C.M.E. in 1995. Morning worship services were held twice a month whereas; Brookins Chapel and Corinth had services once a month. The minister for this church shared all three churches Brookins and New Hope C.M.E. Church. Some of the ministers that were at the church were: Rev. Waddington, Rev. Bevels

Brookins Chapel C.M.E. Brookins Church begins with the Brookins family. The church was located in Saint Paul.

Jake Brookins gave the property for the Church to be built. The church was built around the last 1890s and continued to exist until the 1940's. The building was destroyed during a tornado date is unknown. In the early 1920's Brookins (Brookings) Chapel grew out of the New Hope Church in Malakoff, Texas. Organizers of this church were Thomas, Brookins, McQuirin, and Sisters Brown, M. Brown, Blair and McQuirin. The first pastor was W.M. Douglass on December 7, 1924. According to Mrs. Abrams, who is now 94 as of 2014 she remembers some of the members and the ministers who were sent to pastor the church. Some of those Ministers are:

Elder Rev. Henry
Rev. Brookins
Rev. Griffin
Rev. Henry Q. Dickerson
Rev. Duane McAlister
Rev. Lannie D. Williams
Rev. Tommy Scraters
Rev. Rouselle Jones
Rev. Kalvin Townsend
Rev. Moddie McCalister

With the dwindling membership and physical condition of the structure, Bishop Caesar Coleman condemned this church in 1968. (Tornado destroyed Church) and he asked the members to merge with New Hope.

At Brookins Chapel Before the storm. Was in the 40s I do not know the date

Elder   Rev. Henry
Rev. Brookins
Rev. Griffin
Rev. Henry Dickerson
Rev. Duanoe McCalister
Rev. Lannie William
Rev. Tommy Scraters
Rev. Roshel Jones

~~Rev. Calvin Jones~~
Rev. Calvin Townsel. Malakoff TX.
Rev. Motie McCalister

Members 1. Dewitt Brookins Dec
2. Oliver Thomas Dec
3. Oscar Thomas Sr. Dec
4. Vera Thomas Living
5. Joe Thomas Dec
6. Lonie Thomas Dec
7. Oscar Thomas Jr. Dec
8. Vernon Wingham Dec
9. Generator Wingham Dec
10. Mary Everly Wingham Dec
11. Aria Simpson Brookins Dec.
12 Frank Simpson Dec

Members that belonged to that church who later joined New Hope were:
Dewitt Brookins , Oliver Thomas , Oscar Thomas Sr, Vera Thomas, Joe Thomas, Lonnie Thomas, Oscar Thomas Jr, Vernon Wingham, Generator Wingham, Mary Everly Wingham, Aria Simpson Brookins, Frank Blair, Elsie Blair, and Frank Simpson.

Brookins C.M.E Church

Johnson Chapel AME a lot was given to the church by Zack McCalister. This enabled the church to be built and grow in the community. When the storms hit the community, churches like New Hope and Corinth worship with Johnson Chapel AME. In turn, when the storms destroyed this church they met with New Hope CME until they rebuilt their church.

Gum Creek AME (Co-founders Roderick Barker)

Macedonia Baptist Church
Macedonia grew out of Good Hope Baptist Church. It was organized by Rev. Dan Jackson to service the members that lived across the Creek and wanted to have a church in the Saint Paul Community.
This wood structured church located in Caney City is still standing next door to Troy McCalister's home. The church died out when the members left this community. Some of

the ministers of this church were: Rev. Wallace, and Rev. Robert Wingham. The Church property lot was donated by Rev. Glenn.

Center Union Baptist Church

Old Bethel Church (Jed Adams Site) Helped with the purchase of the Church

Allen Chapel AME Church

Antioch Baptist Church
Antioch Baptist church grew out of Good Hope Baptist Church. It was organized by Bob Smith in 1908 to service a growing Antioch community.

The Colored First Baptist Church history by Maude L. Orr
The Present colored First Baptist Church was originally, the Colored Baptist Church of Malakoff, Texas and from records it is the oldest Colored Baptist Church in the western end of Henderson County. Rev. Monroe F. Jackson, the father of Frank Jackson officially organized this church in November 21, 1894. Rev. Jackson rode a horse from Anderson County to his church until the family moved to Malakoff, Texas. At the time they relocated to this area there was a windmill in the center of town to pump water. A watering trough was there to water horses on what is now known as Terry Street.

The location of the church has remained in the same place, which is now Walker Street just a half block off the Highway 31 West, in the midst of a beautiful group of oak trees on two acres of land in the Peter Tumlinson Survey. Over the years the buildings have changed from time to time from the facing the North to now facing east.

Some of the early families members of this church were: M.F. Jackson, Tom Wilson, John Garrett, Ed. Hicks, Toy Williams, Ella Hicks, Melton Williams, George Hubbard, William All, Sam Mitchell, Will Johnson, Grant Mitchell, W.T. Jackson, General Toliver, Billy Robertson, Jake Redic, Dan Holley, Fannie Marks, Haywood Wingham, Frank Lindsey, Bob Govan, J.D. Shaw, Josephine Garrett. Four of M. F. Jackson daughters married into other Jackson families hence the large number of Jackson in Malakoff, Texas.

The church was purchased from W. Watson and Mary Watson in the amount of 20 dollars paid by Sam Robertson, Governor Wilson, and Monroe Porter trustees of the Colored Baptist Church of Malakoff, Texas. This land was acquired on November 21, 1894.
The Church was renamed to Good Hope Baptist Church. Some of the ministers who pastored there were: Rev. M.F. Jackson, Rev. Andrew Marks, Rev. Talley, Rev. Caldwell, Rev. Clem Smith, Rev. J.W. Hawkins, Rev. Sutton, Rev. J.W. Holmes, Rev F. D. Davis, Rev. C.A. Harris, Rev. J.D. Shaw, Rev. S. R. Roberts, Rev. S. L. Grayson, Rev. Sellus Brown, Rev. C. C. Quarles, Rev. J. L. Sims, Rev. W. S. Mitchell and Rev. Robert C. Hodge.

This Church has gone through several transformations and was later named Good Hope Baptist Church to First Baptist church on Walker Street. The church members of Mt. Olive Baptist along with the Pastor, Rev. S.O.J. Evans met with Good Hope Baptist church and Pastor S.L. Grayson agreed to consolidate for the best interest of the community. With this merger it would allow the membership to grow and become stronger in the community. The years of merger were often tumultuous. Even legal action was used to help mediate difference in the church. With these adversaries the church still stands and is still striving today.

The Mt. Olive Baptist Church
Mt. Olive Baptist Church was another church that grew out of Antioch Baptist Church. In December 28, 1939 the church merged with First Baptist Church.

MILITARY SERVICE

World War I
Larrissie McCalister, Pvt. Co. C, 537 Engineers
Richard Dixie McCalister, Pvt. First Company, First Battalion 165, Depot Brigade and was inducted on August 22, 1918 at Haskell, Texas. His vocation was listed as an Automobile Mechanic. Richard was honorably discharged from the military by reason of Demobilization of Organization per Tel W D Nov 15, 1918.

Charlie McAlister
Robert Lee McCalister Robert L McAllister, private of Company E, Third Regiment Texas Infantry Volunteers, enrolled on April 30, 1898 at San Angelo, Texas. Discharged on February 22, 1899 by reasoning of muster out of the Company

World War II
Elbert McCalister
Venoyd McCalister, Branch Immaterial – Warrant Officers USA, stationed France.-+

Robert E. McCalister, PFC, Pvt-2 13, USAR ARTY, United States Army
Medals: National Defense Service Medal Robert Earl McCalister Army, Private 2, inducted on February 13, 1954. Branch USAR ARTY, Trans Army Res Texas Mil

District. His most significant duty assignment was with the National Defense Service Medal. Assignment 548 AAA Loring Air Force Base Maine

R. D. McCalister, (nickname, monkey) PVT, 47 AM, PH Truck Co. TC WW II
Korean War
Early Hue McCalister, SP 3 (T), United States Army
Medals: Good Conduct Medal
Viet Nam
Joe McCalister US Army
Branches of Services
Army
Early Hugh McCalister
Venoyd McCalister, United States Army
Joe McCalister, United States Army
Brent Curtis McCalister
Travis McCalister
Chester Ray McCalister
Elbert McCalister
Navy
Lowell N. Payne Sr
Cleveland McCalister
Robert Lee McCalister (Morris).

Marines
Air Force
Moddie McCalister
Spatsie McCalister

Schools for African Americans in Henderson County, Texas

There were numerous Public Schools in Eustace, LaRue, Malakoff, Murchison, St Paul, Antioch, Eureka, Jones Farm, Moore station, and Trinidad. Malakoff had the largest population of children which was 745 during the early 1860's. Some of the schools that were designated for Blacks were: (This is a partial list of Black schools from the early 1900's)

Peasand # 36
Teachers: Issac Manion, Trustees: Simpson Thompson, Green Wright, and Richard McCallister

New Hope # 59
Teachers: (1883) J.W. Honston, S.J. Luster, A.L. Simmons, (1884) S.J. Luster.
Trustees: Thomas Henry, Thomas Granville, and Silis Hansy.

Black Teachers from various School Districts1928- 1929
The Colored School, Athens: R. C. Fisher, who was the principal; Mrs. G. H. Swenley, Miss H.B. Massey, Miss E.C. Laurence, Mrs. M.B. Holder, Miss R. H. Stovall.
Malakoff (Colored) A. H. Jones, Mrs. V.A. L. Johnson.
Trinidad (Colored) Mrs. F. C. Pruitt, Ella Leake.
Brownsboro School (Colored) Georgia May Colier and M.E. Ross.
Number 28 ½. Saint Paul, (Colored) J.W. Smother, Odessa Holt, Jessie Mae Dickerson, Mrs. J.W. Smothers.
Number 31 A. Stockard (Colored), Hummie Williams.
Number 37 ½.Eureka (Colored) Georgia Tucker, Lossie Givens.
Number 49 A, Delta (Colored) Berma Dews.
Number 54 A, Fincastle (Colored) Johnnie Howard.
Number 55 Campbell's Chapel (Colored); J.B.Thomas Jr., L.B. Hall, Mae Chum, P.A. Pay, and Mary Walker.
Number 56 A. Pine Forest, (Colored) Bertha Washington.
Number 71 (Colored) J.H. Hilliard, Mrs. J.H. Hilliard.
Cross Roads (Colored) Jessie B. Payne, Azalie Price.

BLACK CEMETERIES

Steen Cemetery 1945
The Antioch community needed another cemetery for burial since they had outgrown the Antioch Cemetery. This cemetery was to serve the people in Malakoff area. According to the committee they could not think of a name for the cemetery and decided to name it after the death of the first individual to be buried there. Steen died first, Zack McCalister died second.

Antioch Cemetery was established in 1883 by purchasing land from John Thomas and Oma Henry to the trustees of the New Hope Methodist Episcopal Church. This cemetery was an active cemetery during that period. Because of the location, and the church relocating, this cemetery no longer held burials at this cemetery. The last person who died there named Mary Street who was buried there in 1969. This cemetery has long served the Black farming community of Antioch. To this day, we are still searching records of the numbers of pioneers and ministers buried here. The earliest known grave was Allen Delorah who died in 1894.

This cemetery is located on Yarabee Ranch Road, an area that use to be called the Yarabee Ranch two and one half miles south of Malakoff.
During the 1970's the cemetery was vandalized and many of the headstones were destroyed and removed. This is so sad that many of our graves were desecrated and left many of us unable to locate our family final resting place.
A push was made to conserve the rich history of Antioch Cemetery by the Texas Historical commission. A Marker dedication ceremony was held on Thursday, July 25, 1985 sponsored by the Antioch-Steen Cemetery Association

Barker Cemetery
Land donated by Armstead Roderick Barker of Gum Creek Community for Burial

Stockard
Slaves of William Richardson (From Picken County Alabama to Texas)

Bethel Cemetery
Descendant of Former Slaves following the Civil War Descendant

North Athens Cemetery
Donated by Abram's Grandparents Charlie and Francis Brown for anyone to be buried
Pauline Westbrook July 23, 1923.
Callie Stoval July 8, 1978

Athens colored cemetery
Emily Anderson (born 1812)
Lizzie Epperson

Sand Flat cemetery
Slaves buried there with William Richardson, wife, two sons, and two grandchildren.
(Slaves) Jude, Dinah, Aunt Mim

Fisher Robinson Cemetery
Fisher Robinson Cemetery was owned by Dilcy Robin's descendants for Slaves in the 1800's. This cemetery is located off of Palestine Highway south now known as Robbins Road. Some individuals who are buried in that cemetery are:
- a) Lizzie Wingfield, Aunt Susan Postell, old man Rube Richardson (son of Della Richardson), (buried near each other). Pearlie, Henry Massey, Jim

Wimbly, Oshmans family, Jeff Criner and wife Tempie Criner, Fred Massey and wife Mattie, Charlie White and Emma White, other members of the Massey family, Jim Wimbly and wife Rozelle, old man Will Graham.

This cemetery records was completed by Marian Westbrook and Mary Ann Perryman through the historical commission of Henderson County in 1980. The individuals buried there were given from interviews of Laura Shafner-Robinson, LeAnna Richardson-Carter, and Mrs. Beulah Larkin's Smith.

CHAPTER 15 Family Reunions

The letter that started the Reunion

The first McCalister Family reunion was held on Saturday, July 25, 1981 at the St. Paul School in Malakoff, Texas. The idea was conceived by Faresa Dawson, Lee A. McCalister, Dr. Joe McCalister, Cleveland McCalister, Reverend Venoyd McCalister and others. All of the family members, who attended this reunion, met and got acquainted for the first time. Everyone enjoyed it and had a good time. Plans were made to repeat this event the next year.

The Letter That Started The Reunions!!!

September 16, 1980

Hello Cuz,

For some time I have thought of writing this letter, but kept putting it off, "no longer". All the family are well, hope this letter will find you and your family the same. "Now!" What's on my mind? Just these two words, "Family Reunion". Think of it for a moment. A McCalister reunion. All of us together. Wouldn't that be something? A copy of this letter will be sent to six other members of the family. I would like for each of you to contact the rest of your sisters and brothers, have them to contact their children. Let's see how everyone feels about it.

Questions should be asked about where it will be, and when. The ones that receive this letter will be on the Committee. Please make your contact as soon as possible, and let me hear from you, so we the Committee may set a date to meet and make plans hopefully for the summer of '81.

Looking forward to hearing from you soon.

Love your cousin,

Cleveland

Cleveland McCalister

11b

P. O. Box 58
Lamesa, Texas 79331
July 23, 1982

McCalister Reunion Group Of 82,

I have recently been asked to serve in the capacity of organizing the program for our McCalister Reunion to be held in Athens, Texas on July 31, 1982.

The purpose of this letter is to find out if you, or any others to be involved, have some special talent area (singing, playing an instrument, dancing, doing a special skit etc.) that you would like to present during that day.
If so, please contact me by telephone - if possible during the early part of next week. Please give the title, length etc. of the number to be presented.
If you are unable to contact me, but have a special number that you would like to present - Just come prepared for it, and notify me at the reunion. . .

We already have several important items for the program, that I consider to be of importance.

I am hoping to see you in Athens and Malakoff on the 31st of July - 1982.

Sincerely,

Lee A. McCalister

Lee A. McCalister
Telephones:
(806) 872-7537 Residence (Anytime other than office hours).

(806) 872-5461 Office (Anytime between 8:00 A.M. and 5:00 P.M. Out for lunch 12:00 - 1:00)

If any of you should have pictures (photos) of the following McCalisters, please bring them:

Isiah   Dixie   Omie
Martha   Early   Willie
Charlie   Lariska   Zack
Cleveland Moddie

Symposium

McCalisters Second Reunion - July 31, 1982
Henderson County Jr. College - (Ballroom)
Athens, Texas

Two or more of the following subjects (or others) may be discussed

1. Possible individual or group McCalister enterprise for the near future in Malakoff, Texas.

2. Your best possibility for becoming financially secure, will hinge on some common sense "Do's and Dont's"

3. Readiness for retirement at any particular age. . . (logical for you). Some very important things to consider. . .

4. Profitable experiences or advise that we would like to share.

5. Getting involved in the educating of your child or children.

I would like to have volunteers available on the 31st. , in-order that we might make a selection of four or six persons to serve on the symposium.
I would like to have a variety of representation: Professional, non-professional, men and women. (Everybody will be able to participate in this effort. . .)

Lee A. McCalister

Malakoff News - Jul 30, 1981   Browse this newspaper
Browse all newspapers »

McCalister Family holds reunion here

Over 150 members of the McCalister family gathered in Caney City at St. Paul Industrial Training School for their first annual reunion. A picnic was held on the lawns of Vee McCalister and Faresa Dawson in Malakoff. Cleveland McCalister, Dayton, Ohio, formerly of Malakoff, organized the reunion.

The occasion was enjoyed by family members in attendance from Washington, D.C., Ohio, Maryland, California, Kansas, Georgia and numerous cities throughout Texas.

Family members present are descendents of the late Isiah and Martha McCalister who were residents of Malakoff in the early 1800's. Some of the positions attained by the McCalisters present at the reunion were film editor, film producer, doctor, attorney, ministers, auditors, realtor, musician, mechanical engineer, teachers, public relations, administrators, supervisors, inspectors and owners of various businesses.

Recognition was given to the oldest member present, Rosa McCalister Garret, (90 yrs. old), Dayton, Ohio, formerly of Malakoff

Reunion Year	Family and Location
1. First Reunion July 25, 1981	St Paul School, Malakoff, Texas
2. July 31, 1982	Henderson County Jr. College, Athens, Texas
3. July 30, 1983	Henderson County, Jr. College Ballroom. Athens, Texas
4. July 28, 1984 Voted to have reunions every two years	Briargate Clubhouse Missouri City, Texas
5. July 19, 1986	Cain Center, Athens, Texas
6. July 16-18 1987	Cain Center Athens, Texas
7. July 16, 1988	El Mina Shrine Temple, Galveston, Texas Sponsor: Early McCalister family
8. July 22, 1989	Cain Center, Athens, Texas Sponsor Charlie McCalister Family
9. July 21, 1990	Woodson Park, Oklahoma City Sponsor Early McCalister
10. July 20, 1991	Cain Center, Athens, Texas Sponsor Zack McCalister
11. July 18, 1992	Cain Center, Athens, Texas Sponsor Cleveland and Omia Family
12. July 17, 1993	Cain Center, Athens, Texas Sponsor Moddie McCalister
13. July 16, 1994	Briargate Clubhouse in Missouri, Texas Sponsor Charlie McCalister family
14. July 15, 1995	Knight of Columbus,

Reunion Year	Family and Location
	Tyler, Texas Early McCalister family
15. July 19-21, 1996	Desoto Civic Center, Dallas, Texas Zack McCalister
16. July 18-21, 1998	Houston, Texas Sponsor Charlie McCalister
17. July 15-17, 2000	Woodson Park Clubhouse, Oklahoma, City Oklahoma Sponsor Early McCalister
Reunion Year	**Family and Location**
18. July 20-22, 2002	Cain Center, Athens, Texas Sponsor Zack McCalister
19. July 16-18, 2004	Suisum City, California Sponsor Early McCalister
20. July 8-9, 2006	Cain Center, Athens, Texas Sponsor Moddie McCalister
21. July 19-20, 2008	Houston, Texas Sponsor Charlie McCalister
22. July 16-18, 2010	Dallas, Texas Sponsor Zack McCalister
July 20-22, 2012	Oklahoma City, Oklahoma, Sponsor Early McCalister
July, 25-27 2014	Houston, Texas Sponsor Charlie McCalister

CHAPTER 16 Looking to the Future

McCalister's are known for their temperament and strong will traits that still continue in the 21st century. We are also recognized by our ability to embrace and love one another as sisters and brothers always putting family first.
Because of the dream and determination of a woman called Mariana and the teachings for her daughter and sons, we still continue a strong family tradition and family traits of loving one another, helping when we need help, stepping in to offer advice, giving a helping hand and accepting constructive criticism.

We must continue to learn from the examples of our fore parents. We must follow their examples since they have left a pattern that was formulated for us to follow for future generations of McC's to become productive individuals.

This blueprint has been a proven fact, because we are still here today as a legacy of our family history. We are Business owners, Doctors, Educators, Ministers, Realtors, Bankers, Brokers, CEO's, Police, Engineers, Inventors, Counselors, Computer IT Programmers', Medical Practitioner of Cancer Researchers, Chemical Engineers, Chemist, Secretaries, Government Officials, State Representatives, Entrepreneurs, Authors, Athletes, and everyday good people.

One thing in particular that I have learned from my Grandmother Vee McCalister is that your name means something. What you do, and how you live reflects back on who you are and what your name represents.

Who YOU are makes the difference, so how does other see you?

Final thoughts....

To the late Cleveland McCalister Jr. families of Dayton, Ohio your father always believed that family comes first and stressed the importance of staying in touch with one another. Cleveland made sure that we know who we were, and we must take care of each other and stick together.

Cleveland loved his family and he loved all McCalister's. He made sure he kept the family notified of death, birth, illness, and location of family members. Because the family was growing, Cleveland discussed reunion ideas with Lee Ander McCalister and they formulated a reunion that would bring all of Isaah descendants together. This reunion set the foundation for future ongoing reunions.

Because of their determination and strong will the first McCalister reunion was held July 25, 1981 in Malakoff, Texas. During this celebration family members from all over came together to meet and greet families while they are still living instead of congregating at funerals. The first genealogical reflection was given by Cleveland McCalister.

Under the direction of the late Cleveland, Lee Ander, Venoyd and Dr. Joe McCalister who is our current president, our family has still continued the tradition of bringing our families together the third week of July.

A special Thanks to Dr. Joe McCalister for continuing to keep the family traditions of a family reunion flourishing. As president of the McCalister Reunion committee he, Deborah Sedberry and I travel to funerals and other additional family programs.

Surname Report

Surname	Count	Male	Female	Earliest	Most recent
McCalister	295	158	137	1817	1987
Betts	161	80	81	1840	1987
Bruce	133	71	62	1800	1966
Templeton	95	46	49	1830	1935
Johnson	92	58	34	1855	1974
Jackson	77	41	36	1809	1945
	69	19	50	1825	1898
Jones	67	36	31	1856	1961
Scott	60	32	28	1835	1953
Brown	59	31	28	1830	1983
Crouch	56	27	29	1845	1954
Dawson	56	28	27	1859	1956

Surname	Count	Male	Female	Earliest	Most recent
Hill	56	27	29	1840	1960
Haynes	52	30	21	1830	1924
Henry	51	18	33	1816	1971
Williams	49	29	20	1870	1971
Wren	49	28	21	1824	1974
Mayfield	47	25	21	1825	1939
King	44	25	19	1854	1964
Blair	43	22	20	1865	1914
Miller	43	22	21	1887	1934
Davis	42	22	20	1850	1978
Eldridge	42	15	27	1828	1957
Smith	37	26	11	1892	1992
Gibson	36	21	15	1908	1989
Granville	34	22	12	1832	1966
Long	31	10	21	1864	1928
Payne	29	13	16	1877	1958
Wiley	27	18	9	1876	1986
Young	27	8	19	1842	1923
Banks	26	17	9	1842	1981
Murray	26	11	14	1838	1988
Graves	25	10	15	1868	1970
Hall	25	11	14	1838	1916
Portley	25	10	15	1826	1938
Surname	Count	Male	Female	Earliest	Most recent
Sloan	25	13	12	1923	1924
Morgan	23	8	15	1842	1937
Campbell	22	9	13	1917	1997
Sibley	22	10	12	1835	1946
Hornbuckle	21	11	10	1821	1927
Andrews	20	11	9		

Surname	Count	Male	Female	Earliest	Most recent
August	19	4	14	1872	1939
Bias	19	15	4	1882	1937
Carter	19	8	11	1929	1965
Hubbard	19	7	12	1869	1949
Huddleston	19	9	10	1877	1922
Shaw	19	11	8	1853	1955
Haines	18	9	9	1830	1908
Traylor	18	10	8	1892	1917
Turner	18	11	7	1870	1870
Blanton	17	9	8	1871	1941
Rogers	17	10	7	1867	1931
Thompson	17	8	9	1871	1936
Deadman	16	4	11	1855	1916
Martin	16	10	6	1850	1958
Taylor	16	9	7	1906	1959
Walker	16	6	10	1887	1949
Washington	16	9	7	1861	1925
Griffin	15	10	5		
Robinson	15	9	6	1848	1899
Sherow	15	9	6	1866	1950
Wynn	15	7	8	1876	1944
Ayers	14	6	8	1825	1904
Crawford	14	8	6	1901	1901
Eubanks	14	5	9	1860	1903
Franklin	14	8	6	1889	1985
Pruitt	14	7	7	1865	1930
Tucker	14	6	8	1884	1969
Cain	13	8	5	1883	1964
Foster	13	3	10	1825	1877

Garrett	13	3	10	1885	1924
Hanes	13	7	6	1862	1928
Lyons	13	6	6	1891	1929
Menefee	13	6	7	1860	1904
Rodgers	12	6	6	1830	1912
Vaughan	12	7	5	1939	1942
Whatley	12	7	5	1855	1904
Winn	12	8	4	1875	1929
Barber	11	7	4	1865	1907
Bowman	11	6	5	1956	1956
Brookins	11	1	10	1874	1919
Elderidge	11	6	5	1892	1930
Green	11	10	1	1890	1970
Jacobs	11	6	5	1853	1909
Ricks	11	5	6	1886	1922
Thomas	11	5	6	1877	1900
Woodard	11	7	4	1956	1956
Alexander	10	2	8	1876	1975
Beverly	10	4	6	1879	1932
Edwards	10	5	5	1874	1874
Ferguson	10	7	3		
Mathis	10	4	6	1884	1909
McCoy	10	7	3	1930	1959
Medlock	10	5	5	1875	1936
Nickerson	10	4	6	1845	1916
Noble	10	5	5	1825	1880
Ross	10	6	4	1879	1926
Stewart	10	6	4	1866	1933
Baker	9	6	3	1903	1909
Coleman	9	4	5	1898	1898
Crosley	9	5	4		

Surname	Count	Male	Female	Earliest	Most recent
Gayle	9	3	6	1901	1923
Harris	9	7	2	1902	1954
McAdams	9	4	5	1834	1888
Ratcliff	9	3	6	1863	1899
White	9	6	3	1931	1931
Bonner	8	6	2	1886	1918
Daniel	8	4	4	1834	1909
Garland	8	4	4	1799	1877
Germany	8	2	6	1939	1950
James	8	6	2	1904	2005
Modester	8	5	3	1879	1941
Trylor	8	3	4	1881	1929
Wingfield	8	2	6	1848	1894
Wingham	8	5	3	1966	1978
Woods	8	3	5	1892	2002
Boyd	7	7	0		
Cannon	7	3	4	1888	1893
Eldrige	7	4	3	1871	1897
Ford	7	2	5		
Hicks	7	6	1	1921	1977
Jr	7	7	0	1910	1995
Langley	7	6	1	1885	1885
McCAllister	7	6	1	1901	1952
Pringle	7	4	3	1949	1949
Ratliff	7	2	5	1853	1853
Richardson	7	4	3	1924	1924
Westbrook	7	5	2		
Anderson	6	5	1	1934	1959
Benton	6	3	3	1976	1976

Surname	Count	Male	Female	Earliest	Most recent
Bronn	6	4	2	1868	1884
Curry	6	3	3	1912	1912
Dansby	6	4	2	1902	1909
Dowson	6	4	2	1883	1902
Greer	6	2	4	1881	1907
Haywood	6	5	1		
Henderson	6	4	2		
Howard	6	4	2	1863	1897
Jiles	6	4	2	1872	1911
Kiser	6	2	4	1867	1927
Mcallister	6	2	4	1902	1945
Nickleberry	6	6	0	1860	1921
Price	6	2	4		
Strickland	6	2	4		
Allen	5	2	3	1813	1923
Alston	5	2	3	1914	1954
Bagby	5	2	3	1840	1879
Booker	5	2	3	1901	1912
Clark	5	3	2	1868	1877
Dockery	5	2	3	1949	1949
Espree	5	3	2	1905	1941
Forte	5	3	2	1967	1970
Fuller	5	1	4	1800	1885
Kennamore	5	4	1	1973	1994
Lee	5	1	4	1918	1918
Modesto	5	2	3	1880	1908
Moore	5	0	5	1891	1965
Moten	5	3	2	1902	1929
Murphy	5	4	1	1974	2000

Surname	Count	Male	Female	Earliest	Most recent
Nickelberry	5	1	4	1850	1898
Prince	5	3	2	1876	1895
William	5	1	4		
Wright	5	2	3		
Barnett	4	4	0		
Barron	4	1	3	1905	1905
Benson	4	3	1		
Bowens	4	2	2	1880	1910
Breland	4	2	2		
Brigham	4	2	2	1898	1937
Byrd	4	3	1	1905	1905
Callahon	4	3	1		
Cooks	4	1	3	1832	1832
Cromwell	4	2	2	1991	1993
Duncan	4	3	1	1916	1916
Ealy	4	3	1	1948	1948
Eldredge	4	2	2	1862	1938
Gooden	4	2	2	1903	1930
Surname	Count	Male	Female	Earliest	Most recent
Grant	4	3	1	1977	1977
Gray	4	1	3	1820	1881
Hibbler	4	1	3	1961	1982
Holiday	4	4	0		
Jordan	4	3	1	1908	1940
Lewis	4	1	3	1917	1946
Luckey	4	3	1	1884	1922
Mackey	4	3	1	1940	1943
McDaniel	4	4	0	1947	1971
Nobles	4	1	3	1830	1891
O'Brien	4	3	1		

Surname	Count	Male	Female	Earliest	Most recent
Powell	4	3	1		
Renfro	4	3	1		
Roberson	4	3	1	1857	1857
ROBISON	4	2	2	1870	1917
Sparks	4	2	2	1933	1933
Sweat	4	4	0	1977	1993
Warren	4	1	3	1880	1899
Wherry	4	2	2	1885	1937
Wilson	4	1	3	1901	1978
Alex	3	1	2	1886	1916
Alford	3	2	1	1969	1969
Armstrong	3	2	1	1873	1899
Bagley	3	0	3		
Barlow	3	2	1		
Boone	3	2	1	1960	1960
Burks	3	2	1		
Butler	3	2	1	1916	1916
Donald	3	2	1	1860	1914
Dunbar	3	2	1		
Ethridge	3	1	2	1934	1934
Felder	3	3	0	1967	1967
Gardner	3	3	0	1963	1963
Givan	3	3	0		
Givens	3	2	1	1879	1892
Glenn	3	0	3	1923	1924
Govan	3	1	2	1895	1919
Grandville	3	0	3	1919	1925
Hawk	3	2	1	1864	1902
Kemp	3	1	2		

Mahdi	3	1	2		
Matthis	3	1	2	1975	1975
McKee	3	2	1	1950	1950
McKinney	3	1	2	1848	1892
Nance	3	2	1		
Neal	3	1	2	1813	1875
Newton	3	3	0	2009	2009
Patterson	3	1	2	1886	1939
Pearson	3	1	2	1929	1929
Perkins	3	2	1		
Portly	3	3	0	1872	1899
Reese	3	2	1	1970	1970
Reynolds	3	2	1	1856	1886
Richards	3	2	1	2005	2005
Robertson	3	0	3		
Royal	3	1	2	1926	1950
Sanders	3	2	1	1880	1880
Sellers	3	2	1	1959	1987
Shell	3	2	1	1890	1890
Sims	3	2	1		
Stephens	3	2	1	1967	2012
Stephenson	3	1	2	1904	1904
Steward	3	1	2	1830	1875
Tillmon	3	3	0	1935	1963
Van	3	2	1	1900	1902
Wallace	3	0	3	1920	1920
Ward	3	2	1	1898	1898
Whitman	3	3	0		
Wofford	3	1	2	1971	1971
Wood	3	1	2	1885	1885
Wynne	3	1	2	1856	1881

Surname	Count	Male	Female	Earliest	Most recent
Bailey	2	1	1	1907	1907
Baulkmon	2	2	0	1967	1967
Blue	2	2	0	1941	1941
Boldens	2	1	1	1900	1930
Buchanan	2	2	0	1938	1938
Burdette	2	1	1		
Burns	2	1	1	1878	1920
Caldwell	2	1	1	1896	1903
Cason	2	1	1	1870	1870
Collins	2	0	2	1908	1952
Cotton	2	2	0	1911	1911
Cranch	2	1	1	1881	1887
Dausby	2	0	2	1899	1910
Dillard	2	1	1	1910	1910
Dorsey	2	1	1		
Elems	2	1	1		
Etienne	2	1	1	1975	1975
Fisher	2	1	1	1933	1933
Fitzpatrick	2	1	1	1912	1912
FOWLER	2	0	2	1903	1903
Frazier	2	2	0	1962	1962
Garner	2	1	1	1923	1923
Garret	2	1	1		
Geter	2	0	2	1910	1910
Gilbert	2	1	1		
Graniva	1	2	1	1	1915	1918
Hampton	2	0	2	1923	1976
Handy	2	1	1	1975	1975
Harrison	2	1	1		

Surname	Count	Male	Female	Earliest	Most recent
Holbert	2	0	2	1902	1905
Holder	2	2	0		
Holland	2	1	1		
Horton	2	1	1	1825	1902
Hunt	2	0	2		
Hutchings	2	2	0	1917	1917
Hutchinson	2	1	1	1940	1940
Ingram	2	1	1	1882	1882
Jenkins	2	2	0		
Lawrence	2	1	1	1911	1911
Linicomn	2	2	0		
Littlejohn	2	2	0	1945	1945
Lock	2	1	1		
Lou	2	0	2		
Love	2	0	2		
Marshal	2	2	0		
Marzette	2	2	0		
McDonald	2	1	1	1896	1898
Mckenzie	2	1	1	1948	1948
Miles	2	0	2	1839	1945
Mitchell	2	0	2		
Muckleroy	2	2	0	1889	1926
Norris	2	2	0		
Osburne	2	1	1		
Owens	2	1	1	1961	1964
Pinkard	2	1	1		
Randall	2	0	2		
Reed	2	1	1	1865	1870
Relerford	2	1	1		

Surname	Count	Male	Female	Earliest	Most recent
Roach	2	1	1	1847	1847
Roper	2	2	0	1894	1894
Roseberry	2	1	1	1908	1908
Rowe	2	2	0		
Sampson	2	0	2	1870	1872
Sedberry	2	2	0	1952	1978
Shaufman	2	1	1	1890	1890
Sheila	2	0	2		
Sherman	2	1	1		
Shield	2	1	1		
Shirley	2	0	2		
Shoulders	2	1	1	1855	1855
Simmons	2	2	0		
Simpson	2	2	0		
Spellmon	2	2	0		
Staggers	2	1	1		
Sterling	2	1	1	1926	1926
Steveson	2	2	0	1930	1932
Street	2	2	0		
Townsend	2	2	0		
Trimble	2	1	1	1909	1939
Walton	2	1	1	1939	1939
Wanda	2	0	2		
Watkins	2	1	1	1891	1911
Webster	2	2	0	1899	1899
Willy	2	1	1	1907	1929
Wrenn	2	1	1	1911	1943
Yolanda	2	0	2		
A.	1	0	1		

Surname	Count	Male	Female	Earliest	Most recent
Adaline	1	0	1		
Aiken	1	0	1		
Aldridge	1	0	1		
Allyson	1	0	1		
Angela	1	0	1		
Ann	1	0	1		
Annie	1	0	1	1893	1893
Anthony	1	1	0		
Austin	1	1	0	1886	1886
B.	1	1	0		
Ballard	1	1	0		
Bank	1	0	1	1898	1898
Barrett	1	0	1		
Battle	1	0	1		
Beasley	1	1	0		
Beasmore	1	0	1		
Beckham	1	1	0		
Bell	1	1	0		
Best	1	1	0		
Beveley	1	0	1	1930	1930
Beverley	1	1	0	1932	1932
Beverly Mccree	1	0	1	1928	1928
Bias-James	1	0	1	1891	1891
Billie	1	0	1		
Billington	1	1	0		
Birdwell	1	0	1	1846	1846
Black	1	0	1	1880	1880
Bland	1	0	1	1872	1872
Blaylock	1	1	0		

Surname	Count	Male	Female	Earliest	Most recent
Bluains	1	1	0		
Bluean	1	1	0		
Bobb	1	1	0		
Body	1	1	0		
Bolton	1	0	1		
Bookan	1	0	1	1888	1888
Brachwaite	1	0	1		
Bradford	1	1	0		
Bruce- Wash	1	0	1	1905	1905
Bruce-Penn-Clark	1	0	1	1908	1908
Brumfield	1	0	1		
Bryant	1	0	1		
Burdine	1	1	0		
Burges	1	0	1		
Burl	1	1	0		
Burleson	1	0	1		
Burnett	1	1	0		
Burries	1	0	1	1963	1963
Burton	1	0	1		
Bush	1	0	1	1876	1876
C.	1	0	1	1880	1880
Cain Parrish	1	0	1		
Cameron	1	0	1	1852	1852
Candy	1	0	1		
Surname	Count	Male	Female	Earliest	Most recent
Canney	1	1	0		
Carol	1	1	0		
Carr	1	0	1	1903	1903
Castille	1	0	1	1978	1978
Cayton	1	0	1	1873	1873

Name					
Chatham	1	0	1		
Chauvin	1	0	1		
Childress	1	1	0		
Clayborn	1	0	1	1924	1924
Clemmons	1	0	1		
Clifton	1	1	0		
Clinso	1	0	1	1893	1893
Colby	1	0	1		
Collier	1	1	0		
Collon	1	0	1	1914	1914
Cook	1	0	1		
Cook-Frazier	1	0	1		
Cooper	1	0	1	1906	1906
Crain	1	1	0		
Crouck	1	1	0	1907	1907
Crutchfield	1	0	1	1870	1870
Cunningham	1	0	1		
Cynthia	1	0	1		
Dalbert1	0	1	1903	1903	
Daniels	1	0	1		
Darty	1	1	0		
Davidson	1	1	0	1956	1956
Daye	1	0	1		
Dean	1	1	0		
Debra	1	0	1		
Denisha	1	0	1		
Dillyer	1	0	1		
Dixon	1	0	1	1908	1908
Doers	1	0	1	1910	1910
Doty	1	0	1		

Surname	Count	Male	Female	Earliest	Most recent
Duckett	1	0	1		
Dudley	1	0	1	1922	1922
Dyfani	1	0	1		
E.	1	0	1	1907	1907
Echols	1	0	1		
Edison	1	1	0		
Edward	1	1	0		
Eldridge Body	1	0	1	1911	1911
Eldridge-Scott	1	0	1	1909	1909
Eldridge-Tucker	1	0	1	1894	1894
Elia	1	1	0	1923	1923
Ella	1	0	1		
Ellinor	1	0	1		
Ellis	1	1	0		
Elnora	1	0	1		
Emmitt	1	1	0		
Epps	1	0	1	1900	1900
Ervin	1	1	0		
Estes	1	1	0		
Evans	1	0	1		
Exzevia	1	1	0		
Falls	1	0	1	1830	1830
Fayrine	1	0	1		
Fitzgerald	1	0	1		
Flemings	1	0	1		
Fletcher	1	1	0		
Floyd	1	1	0		
Fore	1	0	1	1944	1944
Foster Haines	1	0	1	1849	1849

Surname	Count	Male	Female	Earliest	Most recent
Franks	1	0	1		
Fuqua	1	0	1		
Gale	1	1	0	1870	1870
Gamble	1	1	0		
Gaskins	1	1	0	1917	1917
Georgia	1	0	1		
Gibbs	1	0	1	1927	1927
Giddens	1	0	1	1949	1949
Gilkey	1	1	0		
Gite	1	1	0		
Gladys	1	0	1		
Glasco	1	0	1	1993	1993
Graham	1	0	1		
Granvill	1	1	0	1869	1869
Gulick	1	0	1		
Gunther	1	0	1	1967	1967
Gwendolyn	1	0	1		
Haliburton	1	0	1		
Hamilton	1	0	1	1899	1899
Hanns	1	1	0		
Harper	1	0	1	1966	1966
Hartfield	1	0	1		
Haven	1	0	1	1935	1935
Hervey	1	0	1	1858	1858
Hill - Donald	1	0	1	1887	1887
Hinkle	1	0	1		
Hoard	1	0	1	1889	1889

Surname	Count	Male	Female	Earliest	Most recent
Hodges	1	0	1		
Ho-King	1	1	0		
Holloway	1	1	0		
Holmes	1	1	0		
Huddelston	1	1	0	1846	1846
Humphries	1	1	0		
Hunder	1	1	0		
Huston	1	0	1	1874	1874
Irene	1	0	1		
Jaggers1	1	0			
Janice	1	0	1		
Jean	1	0	1		
Jemison	1	0	1	1860	1860
Jemmerson Collier	1	0	1	1919	1919
Jenkens	1	0	1		
Jennerson	1	0	1	1919	1919
Jernigan	1	0	1	1870	1870
Joyce	1	0	1		
Jr.	1	1	0		
Jr.Westbrook	1	1	0		
Judkins	1	0	1	1891	1891
Kennedy	1	0	1	1947	1947
Kinard	1	1	0		
Kinnard	1	0	1		
Kyer	1	0	1	1887	1887
Lambert	1	0	1	1912	1912
Laronda	1	0	1		
Latimer	1	1	0		
Lawson	1	1	0	1856	1856

Surname	Count	Male	Female	Earliest	Most recent
Leblanc	1	1	0	1970	1970
LeBlancs	1	1	0		
Ledet	1	0	1	1951	1951
Liggins	1	0	1		
Lillian	1	0	1		
Liner	1	0	1	1870	1870
Lone	1	1	0		
Lovato	1	0	1	1916	1916
Lucinda	1	0	1		
Lucky	1	1	0	1915	1915
Lundy	1	1	0		
Lusk	1	0	1		
Malone	1	0	1	1809	1809
Mamie	1	0	1	1899	1899
March	1	0	1		
Margaret	1	0	1		
Mark	1	1	0		
Marshall	1	1	0		
Martin-Young	1	0	1		
Mary	1	0	1		
Mattie	1	0	1		
Mays	1	0	1		
Surname	Count	Male	Female	Earliest	Most recent
McAdames	1	1	0	1869	1869
McAdams-Granville	1	0	1	1896	1896
Mcalister	1	1	0	1905	1905
Mcbeth	1	0	1		
McCalaster	1	0	1	1890	1890
McCalister Wilkins	1	0	1	1938	1938
McCalister Williams	1	0	1	1954	1954

Surname	Count	Male	Female	Earliest	Most recent
McCalister-Osborne	1	0	1		
MCClellan	1	0	1		
McCree	1	1	0	1920	1920
McCuller	1	0	1	1864	1864
McLain	1	1	0		
Mcquitinny	1	1	0		
Mears	1	0	1		
Medlock Jones	1	0	1	1900	1900
Mendenhall	1	1	0		
Menifee	1	1	0	1913	1913
Milton	1	0	1	1954	1954
Mobley	1	0	1		
Monie	1	1	0		
Monroe	1	1	0		
Morris	1	0	1		
Morrison	1	1	0		
Mosley	1	0	1	1854	1854
Moss	1	0	1		
Mouton	1	0	1		
Mukenda	1	1	0		
Muller	1	1	0		
Mumphrey	1	0	1	1922	1922
Murrell	1	0	1	1943	1943
Nacole	1	0	1		
Nicholai	1	1	0		
Nickel	1	1	0	1966	1966
Nickelbee	1	0	1		
Norman	1	1	0		
Norrington	1	0	1	1875	1875

Odessa	1	0	1		
Ola	1	0	1		
Overshown	1	0	1		
Pace	1	1	0		
Pam	1	0	1		
Paris Kiser Williams	1	0	1	1890	1890
Parker	1	0	1		
Patrick	1	1	0	1885	1885
Penny	1	0	1		
People	1	1	0		
Peoples	1	0	1	1872	1872
Perry	1	1	0		
Pete	1	0	1		
Pettigrew	1	0	1		
Pilot	1	0	1	1877	1877
Pitts	1	1	0		
Prock	1	1	0		
Prox	1	0	1	1941	1941
Quarles	1	0	1	1873	1873
Queen	1	0	1		
Quita	1	0	1		
Ramirez	1	1	0		
Rankins	1	0	1	1911	1911
Ratcliff-McCalister	1	0	1	1869	1869
Ray	1	0	1	1966	1966
Reashea	1	0	1		
Redic	1	0	1		
Redie	1	0	1	1881	1881
Robinso	1	0	1		
Roosevelt	1	1	0		
Rosie	1	0	1		

Rossum	1	1	0	1891	1891
Rowlett	1	0	1		
Ruth	1	0	1		
Sacrease	1	0	1	1915	1915

Surname	Count	Male	Female	Earliest	Most recent
Sampsom	1	0	1	1847	1847
Sattiewhite-Huert		1	0	1	
Sauls	1	1	0		
Savage	1	1	0	1882	1882
Savannah	1	0	1		
Scrubb	1	1	0		
Sewell	1	1	0	1924	1924
Sharp	1	1	0		
Shelia	1	0	1		
Shelly	1	0	1		
Shelton	1	1	0	1960	1960
Shepherd	1	0	1	1869	1869
Sheri	1	0	1		
Shoulder	1	0	1	1860	1860
Sibly	1	0	1	1872	1872
Sisson	1	1	0	1874	1874
Skelton	1	1	0	1893	1893
Slaughter	1	0	1	1852	1852
Smalley	1	0	1	1878	1878
Spear	1	0	1	1885	1885
Speedy	1	1	0		
Spriggins	1	1	0		
Sr	1	1	0		
Staley	1	0	1	1952	1952

Surname	Count	Male	Female	Earliest	Most recent
Stallworth	1	1	0		
Standley	1	1	0		
Standly	1	0	1	1945	1945
Starks	1	1	0		
Starlight	1	1	0		
Steger	1	1	0		
Stevenson	1	0	1	1908	1908
Stevnson	1	1	0		
Stockam	1	1	0		
Strange	1	0	1	1899	1899
Sutton	1	0	1	1858	1858
Terri	1	0	1		
Thurman	1	0	1	1912	1912
Toles	1	1	0		
Toliver	1	0	1		
Tompson	1	0	1	1902	1902
Trudy	1	0	1		
Tucker-Booker	1	0	1	1915	1915
Van Murphy	1	1	0		
Vance	1	1	0		
Vetrice	1	0	1		
Vinnie	1	0	1		
Vinson	1	1	0		
Wafer	1	1	0		
Wair	1	0	1	1957	1957
Ware	1	1	0		
Waters	1	0	1	1915	1915
Watson	1	0	1	1968	1968
Weaver	1	1	0		

Surname	Count	Male	Female	Earliest	Most recent
Wells	1	0	1	1874	1874
Wheary	1	1	0	1911	1911
Wheatly	1	1	0		
White-Ballard	1	0	1		
Whitefield	1	1	0		
White-Knight	1	0	1		
White-Miller	1	0	1		
Whittaker	1	1	0		
Whittley	1	0	1		
Wilder	1	1	0		
Wilkins	1	1	0	1930	1930
Wilmer	1	0	1		
Witherspoon	1	0	1	1920	1920
Wofer	1	0	1	1982	1982
Womack	1	1	0	1841	1841
Womack Ayres	1	0	1	1860	1860
Woolingham	1	0	1	1844	1844
Wsye	1	1	0		
Surname	Count	Male	Female	Earliest	Most recent
Wyatt	1	0	1	1949	1949
Totals:	4228	2134	2085		

Source Bibliography

1886 Warranty Deed orginal owner.

1890 Tax Rolls Henderson County, Texas.

1910 Census in Shelby County. T624 Roll 1588 page 97 Shelby County.

1910 Fort Ben Census.

1951 Jury List in Henderson County.

Ancestry Family Trees (Online publication - Provo, UT, USA: Ancestry.com. Original data: Family Tree files submitted by Ancestry members.), Ancestry.com, http://www.Ancestry.com.

Ancestry.com and Ohio Department of Health, Ohio Deaths, 1908-1932, 1938-1944, and 1958-2007 (Online publication - Provo, UT, USA: Ancestry.com Operations Inc, 2010.Original data - Ohio. Division of Vital Statistics. Death Certificates and index, December 20, 1908- December 31, 1953. State Archives Series 3094. Ohio Historical Society, Ohio.Ohio Dep), Ancestry.com, http://www.Ancestry.com.

Ancestry.com and The Church of Jesus Christ of Latter-day Saints, 1880 United States Federal Census (Online publication - Provo, UT, USA: Ancestry.com Operations Inc, 2010. 1880 U.S. Census Index provided by The Church of Jesus Christ of Latter-day Saints © Copyright 1999 Intellectual Reserve, Inc. All rights reserved. All use is subject to the limited), Ancestry.com, http://www.Ancestry.com.

Ancestry.com, 1850 U.S. Federal Census - Slave Schedules (Provo, UT, USA, Ancestry.com Operations Inc, 2004), Ancestry.com, http://www.Ancestry.com.

Ancestry.com, 1860 U.S. Federal Census - Slave Schedules (Online publication - Provo, UT, USA: Ancestry.com Operations Inc, 2010.Original data - United States of America, Bureau of the Census. Eighth Census of the United States, 1860. Washington, D.C.: National Archives and Records Administration, 1860. M653, 1,4), Ancestry.com, http://www.Ancestry.com.

Ancestry.com, 1860 United States Federal Census (Provo, UT, USA, Ancestry.com Operations, Inc., 2009), Ancestry.com, http://www.Ancestry.com.
Ancestry.com, 1870 United States Federal Census (Online publication - Provo, UT, USA: Ancestry.com Operations, Inc., 2009. Images reproduced by FamilySearch.Original data - 1870 U.S. census, population schedules. NARA microfilm publication M593, 1,761 rolls. Washington, D.C.: National Archives and Record), Ancestry.com, http://www.Ancestry.com.

Ancestry.com, 1900 United States Federal Census (Online publication - Provo, UT, USA: Ancestry.com Operations Inc, 2004.Original data - United States of America, Bureau of the Census. Twelfth Census of the United States, 1900. Washington, D.C.: National Archives and Records Administration, 1900. T623, 18), Ancestry.com, http://www.Ancestry.com.

Ancestry.com, 1910 United States Federal Census (Online publication - Provo, UT, USA: Ancestry.com Operations Inc, 2006.Original data - Thirteenth Census of the United States, 1910 (NARA microfilm publication T624, 1,178 rolls). Records of the Bureau of the Census, Record Group

29. National Archives, Was), Ancestry.com, http://www.Ancestry.com.

Ancestry.com, 1920 United States Federal Census (Online publication - Provo, UT, USA: Ancestry.com Operations Inc, 2010. Images reproduced by FamilySearch.Original data - Fourteenth Census of the United States, 1920. (NARA microfilm publication T625, 2076 rolls). Records of the Bureau of the Census, Reco), Ancestry.com, http://www.Ancestry.com.

Ancestry.com, 1930 United States Federal Census (Online publication - Provo, UT, USA: Ancestry.com Operations Inc, 2002.Original data - United States of America, Bureau of the Census. Fifteenth Census of the United States, 1930. Washington, D.C.: National Archives and Records Administration, 1930. T626,), Ancestry.com, http://www.Ancestry.com.

Ancestry.com, 1940 United States Federal Census (Online publication - Provo, UT, USA: Ancestry.com Operations, Inc., 2012.Original data - United States of America, Bureau of the Census. Sixteenth Census of the United States, 1940. Washington, D.C.: National Archives and Records Administration, 1940. T627), Ancestry.com, http://www.Ancestry.com.

Ancestry.com, Arkansas, County Marriages Index, 1837-1957 (Online publication - Provo, UT, USA: Ancestry.com Operations, Inc., 2011.Original data - "Arkansas County Marriages, 1838–1957." Index. FamilySearch, Salt Lake City, Utah, 2009, 2011. "Arkansas County Marriages, 1838–1957," database, FamilySearch; from Ark), Ancestry.com, http://www.Ancestry.com.

Ancestry.com, California Birth Index, 1905-1995 (Online publication - Provo, UT, USA: Ancestry.com Operations Inc, 2005.Original data - State of California. California Birth Index, 1905-1995. Sacramento, CA, USA: State of California Department of Health Services, Center for Health Statistics.Original dat), Ancestry.com, http://www.Ancestry.com.

Ancestry.com, California Death Index, 1940-1997 (Online publication - Provo, UT, USA: Ancestry.com Operations Inc, 2000.Original data - State of California. California Death Index, 1940-1997. Sacramento, CA, USA: State of California Department of Health Services, Center for Health Statistics.Original dat), Ancestry.com, http://www.Ancestry.com.

Ancestry.com, California Marriage Index, 1960-1985 (Online publication - Provo, UT, USA: Ancestry.com Operations Inc, 2007.Original data - State of California. California Marriage Index, 1960-1985. Microfiche. Center for Health Statistics, California Department of Health Services, Sacramento, California.Ori), Ancestry.com, http://www.Ancestry.com.

Ancestry.com, History of Henderson County Texas : recording names of early pioneers, their struggles and handicaps, condition and appearance (Online publication - Provo, UT: The Generations Network, Inc., 2005.Original data - Faulk, J. J.. History of Henderson County Texas : recording names of early pioneers, their struggles and handicaps, condition and appearance of the county, advancement and), Ancestry.com, http://www.Ancestry.com.

Ancestry.com, Louisiana Statewide Death Index, 1900-1949 (Online publication - Provo, UT, USA: Ancestry.com

Operations Inc, 2002.Original data - State of Louisiana, Secretary of State, Division of Archives, Records Management, and History. Vital Records Indices. Baton Rouge, LA, USA.Original data: State of Louisi), Ancestry.com, http://www.Ancestry.com.

Ancestry.com, Louisiana, Compiled Census and Census Substitutes Index, 1791-1890 (Provo, UT, USA, Ancestry.com Operations Inc, 1999), Ancestry.com, http://www.Ancestry.com.

Ancestry.com, Minnesota Death Index, 1908-2002 (Online publication - Provo, UT, USA: Ancestry.com Operations Inc, 2001.Original data - State of Minnesota. Minnesota Death Index, 1908-1002. Minneapolis, MN, USA: Minnesota Department of Health.Original data: State of Minnesota. Minnesota Death Index, 1908), Ancestry.com, http://www.Ancestry.com.

Ancestry.com, Missouri Marriage Records, 1805-2002 (Online publication - Provo, UT, USA: Ancestry.com Operations, Inc., 2007.Original data - Missouri Marriage Records. Jefferson City, MO, USA: Missouri State Archives. Microfilm.Original data: Missouri Marriage Records. Jefferson City, MO, USA: Missouri Stat), Ancestry.com, http://www.Ancestry.com.

Ancestry.com, Nevada Marriage Index, 1956-2005 (Online publication - Provo, UT, USA: Ancestry.com Operations, Inc., 2007.Original data - Nevada State Health Division, Office of Vital Records. Nevada Marriage Index, 1966-2005. Carson City, Nevada: Nevada State Health Division, Office of Vital Records.Cla), Ancestry.com, http://www.Ancestry.com.

Ancestry.com, North Carolina, Birth and Death Indexes, 1800-2000 (Online publication - Provo, UT, USA: Ancestry.com Operations Inc, 2005.Original data - Register of Deeds. North Carolina Birth Indexes. Raleigh, North Carolina: North Carolina State Archives. Microfilm.Original data: Register of Deeds. North Carolina Birth), Ancestry.com, http://www.Ancestry.com.

Ancestry.com, Ohio, Birth Index, 1908-1964 (Online publication - Provo, UT, USA: Ancestry.com Operations, Inc., 2012.Original data - Ohio Birth Records. Columbus, Ohio: Ohio Vital Records Office.Original data: Ohio Birth Records. Columbus, Ohio: Ohio Vital Records Office.), Ancestry.com, http://www.Ancestry.com.
Ancestry.com, Selected U.S. Federal Census Non-Population Schedules, 1850-1880 (Online publication - Provo, UT, USA: Ancestry.com Operations, Inc., 2010.Original data - View all sources.Original data: View all sources), Ancestry.com, http://www.Ancestry.com.

Ancestry.com, Social Security Death Index (Online publication - Provo, UT, USA: Ancestry.com Operations Inc, 2010.Original data - Social Security Administration. Social Security Death Index, Master File. Social Security Administration.Original data: Social Security Administration. Social Security D), Ancestry.com, http://www.Ancestry.com.

Ancestry.com, Texas Birth Index, 1903-1997 (Online publication - Provo, UT, USA: Ancestry.com Operations Inc, 2005.Original data - Texas Birth Index, 1903-1997. Texas: Texas Department of State Health Services. Microfiche.Original data: Texas Birth Index, 1903-1997. Texas: Texas Department of State), Ancestry.com, http://www.Ancestry.com.

Ancestry.com, Texas Death Index, 1903-2000 (Online publication - Provo, UT, USA: Ancestry.com Operations Inc, 2006.Original data - Texas Department of Health. Texas Death Indexes, 1903-2000. Austin, TX, USA: Texas Department of Health, State Vital Statistics Unit.Original data: Texas Department of H), Ancestry.com, http://www.Ancestry.com.

Ancestry.com, Texas Divorce Index, 1968-2002 (Online publication - Provo, UT, USA: Ancestry.com Operations Inc, 2005.Original data - Texas Department of State Health Services. Texas Divorce Index, 1968-2002. Texas, USA: Texas Department of State Health Services.Original data: Texas Department of State), Ancestry.com, http://www.Ancestry.com.

Ancestry.com, Texas Marriage Collection, 1814-1909 and 1966-2002 (Online publication - Provo, UT, USA: Ancestry.com Operations Inc, 2005.Original data - Dodd, Jordan R, et. al. Early American Marriages: Texas to 1850. Bountiful, UT: Precision Indexing Publishers, 19xx.Hunting For Bears, comp. Texas marriage information t), Ancestry.com, http://www.Ancestry.com.

Ancestry.com, Texas, Birth Certificates, 1903-1932 (Provo, UT, USA, Ancestry.com Operations, Inc., 2013), Ancestry.com, http://www.Ancestry.com.

Ancestry.com, Texas, Conduct Registers, 1875-1945 (Provo, UT, USA, Ancestry.com Operations, Inc., 2012), Ancestry.com, http://www.Ancestry.com.

Ancestry.com, Texas, Death Certificates, 1903–1982 (Provo, UT, USA, Ancestry.com Operations, Inc., 2013), Ancestry.com, http://www.Ancestry.com.

Ancestry.com, U.S. Cemetery and Funeral Home Collection (Online publication - Provo, UT, USA: Ancestry.com Operations Inc, 2011.Original data Ancestry.com, http://www.Ancestry.com.

Ancestry.com, U.S. City Directories (Beta) (Online publication - Provo, UT, USA: Ancestry.com Operations, Inc., 2011. Ancestry.com, http://www.Ancestry.com.

Ancestry.com, U.S. City Directories (Online publication - Provo, UT, USA: Ancestry.com Operations, Inc., 2010. Ancestry.com, http://www.Ancestry.com.

Ancestry.com, U.S. Phone and Address Directories, 1993-2002 (Online publication - Provo, UT, USA: Ancestry.com Operations Inc, 2005.Original data - 1993-2002 White Pages. Little Rock, AR, USA: Acxiom Corporation.Original data: 1993-2002 White Pages. Little Rock, AR, USA: Acxiom Corporation.), Ancestry.com, http://www.Ancestry.com.

Ancestry.com, U.S. Public Records Index, Volume 1 (Online publication - Provo, UT, USA: Ancestry.com Operations, Inc., 2010.Original data - Voter Registration Lists, Public Record Filings, Historical Residential Records, and Other Household Database Listings.Original data: Voter Registration Lists, Public), Ancestry.com, http://www.Ancestry.com.

Ancestry.com, U.S. Public Records Index, Volume 1 (Online publication - Provo, UT, USA: Ancestry.com Operations, Inc., 2010.Original data - Voter Registration Lists, Public Record Filings, Historical Residential Records, and Other Household Database Listings.Original data: Voter Registration Lists, Public), NAME Ancestry.com ADDR http://www.Ancestry.com NOTE.

Ancestry.com, U.S. Public Records Index, Volume 2 (Online publication - Provo, UT, USA: Ancestry.com Operations, Inc., 2010.Original data - Voter Registration Lists, Public Record Filings, Historical Residential Records, and Other Household Database Listings.Original data: Voter Registration Lists, Public), Ancestry.com, http://www.Ancestry.com.

Ancestry.com, U.S. Public Records Index, Volume 2 (Online publication - Provo, UT, USA: Ancestry.com Operations, Inc., 2010.Original data - Voter Registration Lists, Public Record Filings, Historical Residential Records, and Other Household Database Listings.Original data: Voter Registration Lists, Public), NAME Ancestry.com ADDR http://www.Ancestry.com NOTE.

Ancestry.com, U.S. School Yearbooks (Online publication - Provo, UT, USA: Ancestry.com Operations, Inc., 2010.Original data - Various school yearbooks from across the United States.Original data: Various school yearbooks from across the United States.), Ancestry.com, http://www.Ancestry.com.

Ancestry.com, U.S. World War II Draft Registration Cards, 1942 (Online publication - Provo, UT, USA: Ancestry.com Operations, Inc., 2010.Original data - United States, Selective Service System. Selective Service Registration Cards, World War II: Fourth Registration. National Archives and Records Administration Branch l), Ancestry.com, http://www.Ancestry.com.

Ancestry.com, U.S., Department of Veterans Affairs BIRLS Death File, 1850-2010 (Online publication - Provo, UT, USA: Ancestry.com Operations, Inc., 2011.Original data - Beneficiary Identification Records Locator Subsystem (BIRLS) Death File. Washington, D.C.: U.S.

Department of Veterans Affairs.Original data: Beneficiary Identificatio), Ancestry.com, http://www.Ancestry.com.

Ancestry.com, U.S., Headstone Applications for Military Veterans, 1925-1963 (Provo, UT, USA, Ancestry.com Operations, Inc., 2012), Ancestry.com, http://www.Ancestry.com.

Ancestry.com, United States Obituary Collection (Online publication - Provo, UT, USA: Ancestry.com Operations Inc, 2006.Original data - Ancestry.com, http://www.Ancestry.com.
Ancestry.com, Web: BillionGraves.com Burial Index (Provo, UT, USA, Ancestry.com Operations, Inc., 2013), Ancestry.com, http://www.Ancestry.com.

Ancestry.com, Web: California, Find A Grave Index, 1775-2011 (Online publication - Provo, UT, USA: Ancestry.com Operations, Inc., 2012.Original data - Find A Grave. Find A Grave. http://www.findagrave.com/cgi-bin/fg.cgi: accessed 11 August 2011.Original data: Find A Grave. Find A Grave. http://www.findagrave.com/cgi-), Ancestry.com, http://www.Ancestry.com.

Ancestry.com, Web: Obituary Daily Times Index, 1995-2011 (Online publication - Provo, UT, USA: Ancestry.com Operations, Inc., 2012.Original data - The Obituary Daily Times. The Obituary Daily Times. http://www.rootsweb.ancestry.com/~obituary.Original data: The Obituary Daily Times. The Obituary Daily Times. http:), Ancestry.com, http://www.Ancestry.com.

Ancestry.com, Web: Ohio, Find A Grave Index, 1803-2011 (Online publication - Provo, UT, USA: Ancestry.com Operations, Inc., 2012.Original data - Find A Grave. Find a Grave. http://www.findagrave.com/cgi-bin/fg.cgi: accessed

23 December 2011.Original data: Find A Grave. Find a Grave. http://www.findagrave.com/cg), Ancestry.com, http://www.Ancestry.com.

Ancestry.com, Web: Oklahoma, Find A Grave Index, 1834-2011 (Online publication - Provo, UT, USA: Ancestry.com Operations, Inc., 2012.Original data - Find A Grave. Find A Grave. http://www.findagrave.com/cgi-bin/fg.cgi: accessed 29 February 2012.Original data: Find A Grave. Find A Grave. http://www.findagrave.com/cg), Ancestry.com, http://www.Ancestry.com.

Ancestry.com, Web: Texas, Find A Grave Index, 1836-2011 (Online publication - Provo, UT, USA: Ancestry.com Operations, Inc., 2012.Original data - Find A Grave. Find A Grave. http://www.findagrave.com/cgi-bin/fg.cgi: accessed 19 January 2012.Original data: Find A Grave. Find A Grave. http://www.findagrave.com/cgi), Ancestry.com, http://www.Ancestry.com.

Ancestry.com, World War I Draft Registration Cards, 1917-1918 (Online publication - Provo, UT, USA: Ancestry.com Operations Inc, 2005.Original data - United States, Selective Service System. World War I Selective Service System Draft Registration Cards, 1917-1918. Washington, D.C.: National Archives and Records Admini), Ancestry.com, http://www.Ancestry.com.

Anderson, H. (2000). Larrissie McCalister. (S. M. Wiley, Interviewer)

Anderson, M. (2000). Churches in Henderson County .Brookins, New Hope, and Corinth Christian Methodist Episcopal Church (S. M. Wiley, Interviewer)

Anne Clark, Historic homes of San Augustine (Austin: Encino, 1972)
Athens weekly Review, Athens Texas

Antioch Steen Association with Mr. Homer Ray Trimble, President interviewed in 2010.

Athens Weekly Review August 9, 1928 (Newspaper article 20 years ago. Files from July 30, 1908). Beta.worldcat.org/achiveg.rid/collection/data/704930689. (2012). Retrieved 2012, from Worldcat: http://beta.worldcat.org/archivegrid/collections/

Black Voters Registration List of 1867-1872 Henderson County, Texas. (1867-1872). Athens, Texas, United States of America

Blair, S. (2012). Blair-Richardson-Douglas Union. Athens, Texas.

Bullock, Jessie Payne Family History, Central Texas College for African Americans. Family History Report

Campbell, Charlie T. (2004). Charlie McCalister Family. (S. M. Wiley, Interviewer)

Curry, Willie B. (2000). Richard McCalister's Family. (S. M. Wiley, Interviewer)

Dawson, F. M. (2000). Zack McCalister. (S. M. Wiley, Interviewer)

Deeds Records of Henderson County, Texas 1847-1901 Texas. County Court (Henderson County)
Deed Records of Henderson County, Texas Vol 35, and page 289

Deed Records of Henderson County, Texas Vol 8, and page 127

Deed Records of Henderson County, Texas Vol 238, and page 382

Deed Records of Henderson County, Texas Vol 103, and page 654

Deed Records of Henderson County, Texas Vol 244, and page 83

Find A Grave [database online]; http://www.findagrave.com/, Find a Grave is largely operated by its founder, Jim Tipton.

Griffith, Carolyn, Gregg County, Texas Census, 1900 (Online publication - Provo, UT, USA: The Generations Network, Inc., 1999.Original data - 1900 Gregg County, Texas Census.Original data: 1900 Gregg County, Texas Census.), Ancestry.com, http://www.Ancestry.com.

Griffith, Carolyn, Gregg County, Texas Census, 1910 (Online publication - Provo, UT, USA: The Generations Network, Inc., 1998.Original data - 1910 Gregg County, Texas Census.Original data: 1910 Gregg County, Texas Census.), Ancestry.com, http://www.Ancestry.com.

Henderson County, Texas, marriage indexes, 1860-1942; marriage records, 1847-1942 Texas.

Henderson County, Texas. County Courthouse Probate records

Henderson County, Texas. County Courthouse Warranty Deeds

Henderson County, Texas. County Courthouse 1951 Jury list

Historical Commission, (1871-1897). Henderson County, Texas Marriage Books II, III, IV. Athens,

June 1, 1879 Census records, 1880 census records for Henderson County. page 36, supervisor's dist 1, enumeration dist 31, prec 1

Marriage records of Atoka County, Oklahoma.

Michigan Department of Vital and Health Records, Michigan, Deaths, 1971-1996 (Provo, UT, USA, Ancestry.com Operations Inc, 1998), Ancestry.com, http://www.Ancestry.com.

National Archives and Records Administration, U.S. World War II Army Enlistment Records, 1938-1946 (Online publication - Provo, UT, USA: Ancestry.com Operations Inc, 2005.Original data - Electronic Army Serial Number Merged File, 1938-1946 [Archival Database]; World War II Army Enlistment Records; Records of the National Archives and Records Administration), Ancestry.com, http://www.Ancestry.com.

National Cemetery Administration, U.S. Veterans Gravesites, ca.1775-2006 (Online publication - Provo, UT, USA: Ancestry.com Operations Inc, 2006.Original data - National Cemetery Administration. Nationwide Gravesite Locator.Original data: National Cemetery Administration. Nationwide Gravesite Locator), Ancestry.com, http://www.Ancestry.com.

Ohio Marriage Index, 1970, 1972-2007 (Ancestry.com. Ohio Marriage Index, 1970, 1972-2007 [database on-line].

Provo, UT: Ancestry.com Operations, Inc, 2010.), Ancestry.com, http://www.Ancestry.com.

Texas Marriages Vol 1 page 28, 1868 marriages. Mariah Young and Richard McCalister

Thirteenth Census of the US 1910 Justice Precinct # 2 Hardin County.

Web: Corpus Christi, Texas, Obituary Index, 1940-2010 (Online publication - Corpus Christi Public Libraries.), Ancestry.com, http://www.Ancestry.com.
Web: Dayton, Ohio, Obituary Index, 1850-2010 (Online publication - Dayton Metro Library.), Ancestry.com, http://www.Ancestry.com.

http://www.tshaonline.org/handbook/online/articles/HH/hch13.html (History of Henderson County)

J. J. Faulk, History of Henderson County (Athens, Texas: Athens Review Printing, 1929)Malakoff, Texas Newspaper. (1908, August 9). Athens Weekly Review Dallas Granville. Malakoff, Texas, United States.

McCalister, Vee (2000). Central Texas College for African Americans (S. M. Wiley, Interviewer)

McCalister, Richard (2012) Richards Life. (Rev. Willie Mccalister, Interviewer)

McCalister, Richard (2012) Richards Life. (Zeola Johnson, Interviewer)

McCalister, Zack (2011) Zack McCalister my father (Zeola Johnson, Interviewer)

McCalister, Zack (2011) Zack McCalister my father (Faresa Dawson, Interviewer)

McCalister, Moddie (2008) My Father Venoyd McCalister by Venoyd McCalister (Sheila McCalister, Interviewer)

McCalister, Moddie (September 10, 2003) McCalister-Father and Son by Gloria Pringle (Sheila McCalister, Interviewer)

McCalister, Early (2011) Memories of Burnice by Robert McCalister (Sheila McCalister, Interviewer)
McCalister, Charlie (July 1994) Remembering my Father-Charlie T. Campbell (Sheila McCalister, Interviewer)

McCalister, Larrisse (2000) Larrisse Exploits by Hurley Anderson (Sheila M. Wiley, interviewer)

McCalister, Larrissa (2000) Larrisse by Rev. Willie McCalister (Sheila M. Wiley, interviewer)

McCalister, Larrissa (2000) Larrisse by Faresa Dawson (Sheila M. Wiley, interviewer)

McCalister, Larrisse (2000) Larrisse by Charlie T. Campbell (Sheila McCalister, interviewer)

McCalister, Isaah (October 10, 2010) "Isiah's Horn" Charlie T. McCalister Campbell

McCalister, Martha (2000) Martha Henry's life by Faresa Dawson (Sheila McCalister, Interviewer)

McCalister, Oma (1999) Oma McCalister Granville by Vee McCalister (Sheila McCalister, Interviewer)

Orr, Maude L. Interviews with the following individuals: Frank Jackson on July 10, 1984; Annie C. Wilson, Ernest Wilson on March 5, 1985; Lenora Bailey, Oar Clemons February 27, 1985; L.A. Mitchell, and Carl Anderson on March 3, 1985.

Noble, Harry Jr. "William Garrett Plantation Was near Town" SAN AUGUSTINE TRIBUNE 6 April 1995, pg 6

Noble, Harry Jr. "William Garrett Shared Burdens of Kin" SAN AUGUSTINE TRIBUNE, 20 April 1995, page 6. Probate records, 1846-1936 Texas. County Court (Henderson County)

Retrieved 2012, from Worldcat: http://beta.worldcat.org/archivegrid/collections/

Scholastic Census, 1921-1947 Texas. County Court (Henderson County)

Strain, R. W. (2000). Indexed weekly newspapers: Athens, Texas, forty years (1900-1959), with anthology. Athens, Tex.: Strain Pub. & Seminars.

Strong, M. M. (2006, January). McLemoreStrong Genealogy. Retrieved 2013, from Strong and McLemore History and Ancestry: http://strongfamilytree.org/ Taylor-McCalister, Catherine (July 2004)

The Compiled Records of Henderson County, Texas, collected by John E. Cain on July, 28, 1991.

The Kaufman County TX Gen Web Project Site, history of Texana Ratliff Manion

Website "Cemeteries-of-tx.com" East Texas, Denton, Krum

Website tribalpages.com

William Garrett papers are located at the University of Texas 1832-1834, 1840-1843.

Westbrook, Marian. Written and Tape Recording interview. 1 Jan. 1980. Historical Plans to restore Fisher Cemetery from the Historical Society

William Garrett papers are located at the University of Texas 1832-1834, 1840-1843.

Wynn-McCalister, Mable (2004) Remembering Mable McCalister
1835 Census of Texas

www.ingramcontent.com/pod-product-compliance
Lightning Source LLC
Chambersburg PA
CBHW042055290426
44111CB00001B/19